HOW TO ORGANIZE A CONFERENCE

OTHER BOOKS BY THE SAME AUTHOR INCLUDE:

How to Plan Exhibitions
How to Plan Press Advertising
How to Plan Radio Advertising
How to Plan Direct Mail
Instant Business Letters
Correct Letters
Running a Successful Advertising Campaign
The Business Planner
The Business Environment Made Simple
How to Buy and Run a Shop
Franchising
How to Recruit
How to Win at Job Hunting
How to Win at Interviews
Answer the Question: Get the Job!
The Barclays Guide to Managing Staff for the Small Business
Getting a Result
Managing Your Time

405573

YSTRAD MYNACH COLLEGE

How to Organize a Conference

IAIN MAITLAND

Gower

Published by
Gower Publishing Limited
Gower House
Croft Road
Aldershot
Hampshire GU11 3HR
England

Gower
Old Post Road
Brookfield
Vermont 05036
USA

Iain Maitland has asserted his right under the Copyright, Designs and Patents Act
1988 to be identified as the author of this work.

British Library Cataloguing in Publication Data

Maitland, Iain
  How to Organize a Conference
  I. Title
  060.68

405573
N658· 4562

  ISBN 0–566–07552–0

      Library of Congress Cataloging-in-Publication Data
Maitland, Iain.
  How to organize a conference/Iain Maitland.
      p.   cm.
  Includes index.
  ISBN 0–566–07552
  1. Hospitality industry—Handbooks, manuals, etc. 2. Congresses and conven-
tions—Planning—Handbooks, manuals, etc. 3. Meetings—Planning—Handbooks,
manuals, etc. I. Title.
TX911.2.M35 1995
647.94--dc20   95-1062
                                                                         CIP
Typeset in Palatino by Raven Typesetters, Chester and printed in Great Britain
at the University Press, Cambridge

To Tracey, Michael and Sophie

Contents

List of Figures

Preface

How to Organize a Conference is written for you – the panic-stricken
executive who has been handed the responsibility of staging a successful event. You are now reading this in the hope that it will give you
some of, or even all, the answers. No such luck! What it does offer is
better than that, though. With the aid of its unique blend of questions,
checklists and illustrative documents, you will be able to provide your
own answers to meet your specific needs. They will enable you to:

- set appropriate objectives for your conference;
- establish a realistic budget;
- draft a winning programme;
- plan a sensible schedule to adhere to;
- choose the right venue;
- bring in first-class speakers;
- invite suitable delegates;
- publicize your conference effectively;
- employ first-rate outsiders to assist you;
- speak well in public;
- use equipment satisfactorily;
- stage rehearsals properly;

–   manage the event successfully;

–   follow through to further success.

Of course, this distinctive format means that you will have to work harder and think more than you do when reading a conventional book, but it is worthwhile – by the end of this book, you will have generated a wealth of knowledge and information suited perfectly to your own particular circumstances. In effect, you will have created a handbook written specifically for you – the calm and professional executive who can now run an outstanding event.

Iain Maitland

Acknowledgements

I wish to thank these individuals and organizations for their assistance during the compilation of this book: Margaret Billingham, Birmingham Marketing Partnership; Terry Billingham, Connect; Nina Bond, Oatlands Park Hotel; John Charlton, Conferences and Exhibitions Diary; Steve Charlton, The Griffin at Leeds; Karen Charter, Association of Conference Executives; Heather Chester, Meetings Industry Association; Anne Collins, Holiday Inn Worldwide; Jean Cousins, Swansea Institute; Anne Davies, Great Yarmouth Marina Centre; Jackie Delaney, Losehill Hall; Robert Enefa, The Conference People; Caroline Griffiths, Merseyside Tourism and Conference Bureau; Claire Healy, Aubrey Park Hotel; Susie Helme, *Conference and Exhibition Fact Finder*; Albert Kemp, Insurex Limited; Frank Kuster, Park Hotels; Paul Lewis, Harrogate International Conference Centre; Patricia Moore, British Tourist Authority; Jean Neville, Benn Business Information Services Limited; Joyce Proia, Bolton Institute; Nick Robinson, The Marketing Guild; Tony Rogers, British Association of Conference Towns; Catherine Warrington, Greater Manchester Visitor and Convention Bureau. Special thanks are due to those organizations that allowed me to reproduce their documents within the text.

IM

1

Setting Objectives

To begin with, you must be absolutely clear about what you want to achieve from your conference. Perhaps the easiest and most efficient way to do this is to ask yourself numerous 'who, what, when, where, why and how' questions. Answering them fully and accurately should provide you with a framework of objectives to work within and towards as you organize the event.

Who?

First, give some thought to who should be at the conference – speakers, delegates – and the numbers involved. Start by addressing the following questions.

Who do you want to speak at the event?

In-house speakers are one option – perhaps the managing director, marketing director and/or the sales director. The top salesperson might be an appropriate choice. Decide how many in-house speakers you think you should use. The alternative is to employ outsiders – a specialist in the field or a celebrity who can also act as an attraction to delegates. Again, decide how many you should commission.

Who do you wish to attend the conference?

There are various possibilities – in-house staff, salespeople, and administrative employees among others. Should everyone come along or just a selected number? Should you invite their partners? It may be appropriate to invite outsiders such as sales intermediaries, independent sellers, prospective buyers, media representatives, professional associates or members of trade bodies. How many should be invited – anybody from anywhere or just the chosen few? Should you invite partners as well?

What?

Next, turn your attention to the type of conference you are going to set up and what you want your speakers and delegates to do during and after the event. Consider these issues in particular.

What type of event are you organizing?

Sales   Is the intention to review sales results, to set new targets or to motivate delegates to work harder and better?

Incentive   The objective could be to reward the best sellers, inspire them to improve themselves even further, or to encourage others so that they can attend next time.

Promotional   Do you want to launch new products and services? To publicize revamped goods and services?

Press   Is the aim to give news and information to the media? To obtain free publicity?

Trade   Is the purpose to discuss market activities and trends? To reach a trade agreement?

Training   Do you want to show how to use products and services? To demonstrate how to carry out tasks and duties?

The event could perhaps be a combination of these types – sales *and* training, for instance, or trade *and* press.

What sort of message do you want your speakers to convey?

The message might be informative – about sales figures to date, for instance – or it might be inspiring, with the aim, perhaps, of motivating delegates to do their very best, or it might be persuasive, to encourage them to buy or publicize products and services. Alternatively, you may wish to put across either a provocative message in order to stimulate debate, or an ambiguous one to encourage delegates to think for themselves.

What do you want the delegates to do?

Is your aim to encourage delegates to: maintain or improve their performance; work as hard as they can; purchase your revised goods; publicize your firm and its activities; agree on a common approach to market problems; or do a job differently?

When?

Timing is an aspect which is often overlooked or ill-considered. Step back and consider when the event should be held. Don't simply accept the dates suggested by your managing director (or whomever).

When do you wish to stage the conference?

Do you want to hold it in three, six or nine months time? One year ahead – or more than that? Do you have enough time to organize everything properly? What will happen if you don't? If there isn't enough time would it be wiser to postpone the conference so it can be truly successful?

When do you *not* want to hold the event?

Do you wish to hold it during the busiest sales periods, perhaps, or when competitors traditionally launch new or improved ranges, or possibly on the busiest local news days? Should it be at the most demanding trading times? When employees are most often away on summer holidays? Obviously *all* these options should be avoided!

Where?

Obviously the question of where the event should be staged is as significant as the question of its timing. There are many alternatives available and it is important to make the correct choice. The following preliminary questions will help you to do that.

Where do you wish to run the conference?

Your own premises, head office or a regional office are possibilities. You could also consider an hotel or purpose-built conference centre; a college or university; or somewhere unusual, such as a theatre, stately home, racecourse, football stadium, theme park, castle, ship – a lighthouse, even.

Where would participants want the conference to be held?

Would the speakers want somewhere unusual? Accessible? Pleasant? Modern? Up to date? What else? Would the delegates have the same wants as speakers?

Why?

'Why?' is almost certainly the most crucial question that needs to be asked at this stage. Don't ignore or underestimate it. You must be able to answer it well if you are going to proceed with your plans.

Why are you staging a conference?

Is 'because we always do at this time of year' a good enough purpose? It could be a huge waste of time and money if it is held for this reason alone. Are you staging it because it is the quickest and easiest way of putting across your important message to many people in a friendly and personal manner? That's a better reason.

Consider carefully if a conference is really necessary. Are there less time-consuming and costly ways to achieve the same goals – perhaps a sales report, a promotional brochure or a press release? If there are, think again!

How?

If you decide to press ahead, ask yourself several 'how' questions to complete your framework of objectives. The following are especially relevant.

How should the event be conducted?

Should there be one speaker talking to delegates *en masse* or several speakers running various smaller sessions? Do you want speeches, presentations, demonstrations and discussions? Consider whether this is to be just a business programme with hard work and no play. Or you may want fun and games – a combination of a business and a social programme, possibly with something for speakers' and delegates' partners to do as well.

How long should the conference last?

What is its usual duration? This does not mean this is the right length. Think about what you have to convey to delegates and how you intend to do it. Can you strike a balance to make it short enough to maintain delegates' interest and limit your costs, but long enough to cover everything thoroughly?

How does the event fit into your overall marketing programme?

Be clear whether it is a stand-alone conference, a one-off event that is separate and distinct from your other activities. Alternatively it could be part of a wider campaign – just one aspect of other ongoing advertising and marketing work.

Of course, all these questions are interlinked. For example, who you invite will depend largely on what type of conference you are staging. For example, if it is an incentive event you may want only the best salespeople to attend in order to motivate the others to work harder and do better so that they can come along on another occasion. Thus, when answering any given question, you need to be conscious of the influences on it of all of the other variables.

Recommended reading

Rouillard, L.A. (1994), *Goals and Goal Setting*, Kogan Page, London.

2

Establishing a Budget

Once you have clarified your objectives, move on to establish a budget for the conference so that everyone involved is aware of what can be spent and in which areas. So far as is possible at this early stage list all the likely areas of income and expenditure before going on to compile both the budget and a cashflow forecast leading up to the event.

Listing likely income

Consider where the money is coming from to fund this event. There may be a number of sources of finance available to you. Be aware of these and of how much money they might yield. Consider the following possible sources in particular.

Is there any money available from prospective sponsors?

If you are staging a trade-related conference, a professional association may provide funds and would be worth approaching. You could try a local Training and Enterprise Council or another organization if you are arranging a training event. If you are attracting delegates from overseas you could contact the Department of Trade and Industry. Approach any other organizations or individuals who might stage a complementary exhibition or similar marketing activity alongside your own conference.

Do you intend to sell tickets to delegates and/or their partners?

It would probably not be appropriate to sell tickets to internal delegates. What about their partners, though – should you charge them if they wish to attend? Would it be fitting to sell tickets to external delegates and/or their partners? Consider whether it would dissuade some (or even all) of them from coming. On the other hand, it could make the event seem more attractive – it might seem worthwhile *because* it costs money but worthless if it is free.

Is financial support available from other sources? Directly or indirectly?

Tourist boards may help with promotional activities; free tourist information brochures, leaflets, maps and so on which will save you money. Convention bureaux may provide mailshots on your behalf and similar help with promotional tasks. They might even hold a reception for you. They could save money for your firm.

Is your business going to finance the event?

Every single, last penny? If you are financing only part of it, decide where the rest is to come from: sponsors, delegates, partners or other sources. Clarify which department is going to provide the funds: marketing, sales, public relations, personnel, more than one department or all of them.

Detailing possible expenditure

Then look at where the money must be spent in order to stage a successful conference. Many different areas can be identified. Be conscious of these and how much money you may have to spend on them. Study the following areas.

Have you thought about the cost of hiring a venue?

Take into account both the basic hire charge – is it a fixed price or on a per capita basis? What is the cost of add-ons – for example, facilities, services, equipment hire, technicians, set up and dismantling charges.

If overnight accommodation is to be included, there will be the cost of room charges, extras, facilities and services. These costs will not be incurred, of course, if you use your own premises, facilities, services and equipment instead.

What about speakers? Will they need paying? Do their partners have to be invited too?

Consider the cost of finding speakers, approaching and negotiating, writing, updating, telephoning and confirming. In addition, consider their fees for attending – are they specialists or (expensive) celebrities? You will need to meet their travel and accommodation expenses – will they be coming a long distance? Do they expect first-class travel? Are they used to first-rate accommodation? They will also incur miscellaneous expenses. Do they expect you to pay their drinks bill at the end of the event, for instance? Or for anything else?

How about delegates? Will they cost you money? What about their partners? Will you have to pay for them?

What is the cost of inviting them, finding delegates, obtaining mailing lists, printing invitations, posting them, writing again and telephoning? Include travel and accommodation costs. Are they travelling some way? Do they expect standard-class travel and accommodation or more than that? There may be other expenses, such as free use (for them) of hotel facilities and services. Limit these expenses as far as possible. Can you charge fees to cover some of (or even all) these costs?

Have you considered the cost of publicizing the event? Will you need to do this? If so, how extensively?

If you intend issuing press releases take into account the cost of paper, envelopes, postage, and the expense of faxing the releases to newspapers and magazines. Mailing out letters can incur expenses as it involves buying and maintaining a mailing list, stationery, postage, fax costs and inserts such as product samples and sales literature. If you are thinking of advertising in the press, compare the cost of boxed display advertisements and classified advertisements running line after line under a general heading.

What about the expense of bringing in outside individuals and organizations to help you?

Consider the following potential expenses.

Printing or supplying publicity material   Pre-conference documents, maps, 'What's On' guides, badges, conference documents, programme of activities, printing costs, packaging, postage, spares.

Transporting participants and goods   To cover speakers, delegates, partners, stage sets, display stands, equipment such as overhead projectors, televisions, camcorders?

Decorating the venue   Signs, banners, sashes, flower arrangements, either inside the premises or outside in the car park.

Hire charges   For equipment, facilities and services which are not available at the venue or not up to scratch.

Security   Personnel on the door to check badges, turn away rivals and watch comings and goings to prevent expensive items from being stolen (it often happens).

Catering arrangements   A reception, breaks, lunches, dinners, a banquet, all laid on at the venue, by outside caterers.

Social activities   Entertainment, either inside or outside the venue, for partners while speakers and delegates are occupied and for all participants after working hours.

Insurance   In case the conference is cancelled or abandoned. Check what else should be insured and what insurance you have. You may need more in case of injuries to your employees or third parties, or damage to property.

How about rehearsals? Are these expensive?

If a rehearsal is to be held, the costs must be budgeted for. These may include: fees, travel and accommodation expenses for outside speakers; additional charges for the venue and any facilities and services required; the costs of any facilities and services provided by outside suppliers; overnight accommodation costs if necessary.

What about the programme itself? Is this costly?

Check that the fees for outside speakers are appropriate and calculate travel, accommodation and miscellaneous expenses for speakers, delegates and their partners. Calculate the cost of hiring the venue, ensuring that the costs of any add-ons are built into the figures. If outside suppliers and organizations are involved, add in their costs, updating this figure if the rehearsal demonstrates that any extra facilities will be needed for the event itself.

What costs might be incurred after the conference?

If a report is to be published for internal or external distribution, costs will be incurred for printing, packaging, postage and spare copies to be retained. You may wish to subscribe to trade publications, magazines and directories to help you stay in touch with the changing industry, or join trade bodies to maintain contact and/or take advantage of benefits available to members. If you will be enrolling staff on training courses to improve performance, calculate the costs of fees, travel, accommodation and sundry expenses.

Are there any other expenses that should be added to the list?

You may wish to make an allowance for both your time and effort and that of your colleagues, employees and other staff who have to cover for you while you are organizing the event. When costing the conference itself, remember to take inflation into account – today's prices may have risen by the time the conference is held in a year or eighteen months' time. Check also that you have allowed for value added tax and for any possible change in the rate between now and the conference date.

Compiling the budget

When you have drawn up (potentially long) lists of the possible areas of income and expenditure, pull together some figures and compile a budget which can be referred to by everyone as and when required. The budget form reproduced as Figure 2.1 on pages 12 to 13 may be helpful to you.

		£
INCOME		
Sponsors:	Your professional association	
	Training and Enterprise Council	
	Department of Trade and Industry	
	Fellow exhibitors	
Delegates:		
Partners:		
Other sources:	Tourist board	
	Convention bureau	
	Other	
Self:		
	Total income	—————
Venue:	Hire charge	
	Add-ons	
Overnight accommodation:	Room charge	
	Extras	
Speakers and partners:	Initial costs (finding, etc.)	
	Fees	
	Travel, accommodation	
	Miscellaneous extras	
Delegates and partners:	Initial costs (finding, etc.)	
	Travel, accommodation	
	Other expenses	
Publicity:	Press releases	
	Mailshots	
	Press advertisements	
	Other	
Outside assistance:	Publicity material	
	Transport	
	Decorating	
	Equipment hire	
	Security	
	Catering	
	Social activities	
	Insurance	
	C/fwd	—————

Figure 2.1   Budget form

```
                                              b/fwd    £
Rehearsals:         Speakers
                    Venue
                    Outsiders
                    Overnight accommodation

Programme:          Speakers, partners
                    Delegates, partners
                    Venue
                    Outsiders
                    Overnight accommodation

Post-conference     Conference reports
activities:         Trade publication subscriptions
                    Trade body membership
                    Training courses


                                 Total expenditure  _____
                                                    _____
```

Figure 2.1   Budget form (concluded)

What is your financial aim regarding the conference?

If you are trying to make a profit, how much are you aiming for? Alternatively, are you happy to just break even on this occasion? If you are willing to run the event at a loss, you should know by how much and how you will offset any losses. You could do this through increased long-term sales from more motivated sales staff, perhaps, or by well-trained employees becoming more productive.

Can you finalize your likely sources of income?

How much money will be made available to you by sponsors and what will you have to do in return? How much can you charge delegates and partners and how many do you expect to attend? Assess what you will have to offer for them to consider it a value-for-money deal. What exactly are other sources going to do for you and how much money will this save? Are you happy with what they are planning to do on your behalf? How much of the finance is coming from within your own resources, and does the relevant department know about this?

Can you confirm the probable areas of expenditure?

What are the most relevant areas to you? The venue, the speakers, the delegates, publicity, promotional materials, transport, decorations, equipment hire, security, catering, insurance, rehearsals, business *and* social activities, conference reports and additional training?

Which are the less relevant areas? The venue (are you staging the event at head office?) Speakers (will you be using in-house speakers?) Publicity (because it is an in-house conference)? What else?

Can you write down some rough-and-ready figures for each area?

You may be able to estimate costs by drawing on your own business knowledge and experience – for example if you have hired a venue before, made travel arrangements or booked overnight accommodation. Colleagues may be able to help. Perhaps marketing colleagues can offer advice on mailing to delegates, advertising in the press and booking entries for directories. Your business contacts could help you, too. Existing suppliers may be able to quote for printing, decorating, equipment hire and insurance. Trade associations, such as one of the many bodies in the conference industry (Association of Conference Executives (ACE), British Association of Conference Towns (BACT), Connect, Meetings Industry Association (MIA)) may also be of use – see 'Useful Contacts', page 219.

What type of budget should you set at this stage?

You could choose one which includes a minimum figure below which corners will have to be cut, sometimes drastically, and above which the conference can be run smoothly and successfully. Or you might opt for one which also incorporates a maximum figure which, if exceeded, suggests that money is being spent unnecessarily in some areas and, if underspent, indicates that sufficient funds are available to organize a winning event well – in short, a loose and flexible budget which can be adapted as and when required.

Composing the cashflow forecast

Often overlooked – until the money runs out – is the importance of preparing a cashflow forecast, showing when monies will be made available and have to be paid out on a month-by-month basis. You do need to be conscious of your financial position every step of the way. Figure 2.2 on pages 16 to 17 shows a cashflow forecast form which may be of assistance to you.

When will income be received? Other financial help?

From sponsors   Will money be paid upfront and as early as possible?

From delegates and their partners   Will they pay prior to the conference or upon registration at the event?

From other sources   Will they pay in advance or at the time?

From your own firm   Do the relevant departments know when funds are required? Will you receive them automatically? Will it be a struggle to obtain them on time?

When will expenditure be incurred?

The venue   Is a deposit required? If so, how much is it and when should it be paid? What is the remaining balance and when is it due? Don't forget add-ons, facilities and services. Are these to be included with the deposit or with the balance, or are they to be billed separately after the event?

Speakers   What are the costs of finding and inviting outside speakers? Are their fees to be paid in advance or after the event? When are their travel, accommodation and other expenses to be paid?

Delegates   What are the costs of finding and inviting delegates? Are their travel, accommodation and miscellaneous costs to be paid in advance or at a later date?

Publicity   What are the costs of issuing press releases and mailing letters and when are these costs likely to be incurred? When will press advertisements be booked and paid for?

Bringing in outsiders?   Will publicity material be paid for on receipt or will 30 days' credit be allowed? When will transport be paid for? When is payment due for the hire of decorations and equipment? Will this

	Month			Month			Month			Month			Month			Month	
	Estimated	Actual		Estimated	Actual		Estimated	Actual		Estimated	Actual		Estimated	Actual		Estimated	Actual
Income																	
Sponsors																	
Delegates/Partners																	
Other sources																	
Self																	
Total Income (A)																	
Expenditure																	
Venue																	
Overnight accommodation																	
Speakers/Partners																	
Delegates/Partners																	
Publicity																	
Outside Assistance																	
Rehearsals																	
The programme																	
Post-conference activities																	
Other																	
Total expenditure (B)																	
Net cashflow (A–B)																	
Opening Balance																	
Closing Balance																	

Figure 2.2 Cashflow forecast form

16

Month		Month		Month		Month		Month		Totals
Estimated	Actual	Estimated	Actual	Estimated	Actual	Estimated	Actual	Estimated	Actual	

Figure 2.2 Cashflow forecast form (concluded)

follow the normal practice of a deposit and a balance after the event? Will advance payment in full be required for security, catering, social activities and insurance?

Rehearsals   Are the costs of the speakers, venue, outside suppliers and overnight accommodation included elsewhere in the budget, or are they to be billed separately? Should these costs be paid at the time of the rehearsal?

The programme itself   Are the costs of the speakers, delegates, partners, venues and outside suppliers and organizations incorporated into your previous calculations for both business and social activities?

Post-conference activities   What are the costs of compiling a report? When are subscriptions to trade journals and joining fees for trade associations due? If training courses are to be used, are the fees payable in advance or on arrival?

Are there any substantial surpluses at any time? If so, what should you do?

Your options are to pay cash on collection to negotiate a better price, settle a bill earlier than expected or obtain a prompt payment discount. These will all help to improve your reputation.

Are there any shortfalls at any stage? If so, what will you do?

You can try to obtain income earlier than expected from sponsors, delegates, other sources or your own firm. Alternatively, you could delay payments. The effects of this might be that you have to renegotiate deals, lose early settlement discounts, damage your reputation, or lower your credit limit. Is this wise?

Recommended reading

Hopkins, L. (1993), *Cashflow and How to Improve it*, Kogan Page, London.
Maitland, I. (1995), *Budgeting for Non-financial Managers*, Pitman, London.
Secrett, M. (1993), *Mastering Spreadsheet Budgets and Forecasts*, Pitman, London.

3

Drafting Your Programme

Next, sketch out a programme for your conference. Even though this will only be a provisional draft to be amended and improved as you proceed, it will help you to focus your mind on the event and to gather your thoughts together about planning a schedule, choosing the venue, bringing in speakers and so on. Think about having a theme, before going on to create and devise business and social activities which will comprise a well-balanced programme.

Having a theme

Some conferences have a particular theme. It may range from a clear and self-explanatory one such as 'Hobsons Sales Review of 1996' and 'The Wayliner – Launching an Innovative New Product' to the rather more obscure and abstract 'Doing it Right', 'Winning Ways' and the like. If you are interested in having a theme, think through the following questions before reaching a decision.

What should be the main purpose of a theme?

This could be to persuade speakers and delegates to come to the conference or to encourage others to publicize it. Or it could be to help to put across your key message – 'Work harder and better!', 'Buy these goods!', 'Promote them!', 'Let's reach an agreement!' and so on. If the purpose is to build a solid, lasting impression of the event consider why this is important. Is it to keep sellers working well, for instance, or to continue buying or promoting?

When would it be most useful?

The theme might help to bring in speakers for the conference. It could help attract delegates. It might be useful when you are publicizing the event – you could refer to it in press releases, mailshots and advertisements to convey your key message. In the build-up to the conference you could mention it again in pre-conference documents, and emblazon it across decorations for the venue. Perhaps it would be most useful at the event itself, repeated in speeches, discussions, and question and answer sessions. It may even be drawn into the social activities in some way, with entertainments that reflect the theme, building up a solid impact. After the event it could be incorporated in any post-conference reports for delegates to maintain a long-lasting impression.

When might a theme be less relevant or even harmful?

An unnecessary theme might do more harm than good. Consider whether you need to have a theme to sell this event. Perhaps speakers and delegates will want (or have) to come along anyway. Do you need a theme to put over a memorable message or might good speakers be capable of doing this anyway? Another danger lies in having too clever a theme. It is possible to be too obscure and confusing. A vague theme – 'Being a Winner', 'Getting There' – could put people off rather than appeal to them. It is possible to become too dependent on a theme; if it is referred to endlessly and at every opportunity it can eventually become tedious.

What is the 'right' theme?

The correct theme for you may be a specific one which sums up your main message in a clear and concise manner, is easy to understand and avoids being too clever or obscure. It may be best to use an underlying theme – something which is referred to regularly but not too frequently.

Creating business activities

Having thought about the type of conference you are arranging and how it should be conducted, you will probably have some firm ideas about what will be included within your business activities. Nevertheless, give them further thought now so that a preliminary timetable can be drafted out.

Is this a sales conference?

If so, do you need to cover past sales figures, future sales targets or maybe selling methods? There could be other topics to be covered – those new products which are to be introduced soon or an acknowledgement of the success of key salespeople, for example. Awards can be presented to the best salespeople in the firm.

Think about how these topics should be handled. There are several possibilities. One person might make a speech about past sales figures to all of the delegates, followed by a discussion. The same person could talk about sales targets and selling methods, and hold a question-and-answer session. There might be several sessions where experts demonstrate new products to groups of delegates and then perhaps allow the goods to be examined and tested.

Consider the order and length of the sessions you might have. Short and sweet sessions with plenty of breaks keep everyone fresh and interested. This is far better than long and endless ones with few breaks which exhaust and bore everybody!

Is this an incentive event?

This is much the same as a sales conference, albeit with fewer delegates and in a more exotic location. Consider the approach, and whether there should be speeches, discussions, question-and-answer sessions, demonstrations and presentations. There could be a greater emphasis on inspirational speeches and awards presentations.

Think about the order and length of the various activities. A similar order to a sales conference may be appropriate, with differing lengths of presentations. Perhaps you could allow more time for relaxation or possibly to reward those successful sellers?

Is this a promotional conference?

Decide what should be incorporated in this event. For example: information about a new product; technical data; reasons for its launch; its strengths; unique selling points; why delegates should buy, use or promote it; details about a revised product range (broader or in greater depth); another service; facts and figures; reasons for its introduction; its pluses; special features; why it should be purchased; boosting the firm's image and so on.

You can tackle these areas in various ways: with an introductory speech about the new product, revised range or additional service; with questions and answers from and to the floor; with demonstrations of the various products and perhaps a chance for delegates to touch, feel, examine and test the goods.

Think too about the sequence of the items, their length and whether they should be short on theory and long on practice – with a brief and concise speech, limited time for questions and answers and plenty of time for demonstrating and examining the products.

Is this a press conference?

You should probably cover similar topics to those for a promotional event, but should aim at media representatives rather than prospective sellers, intermediaries or buyers. The approach could include a speech, discussion, questions and answers, a demonstration, an examination and almost certainly an increased number of freebies for journalists, to obtain press coverage.

Consider the order and length. A speech, questions and answers, a demonstration and an examination may be a suitable sequence. Alternatively, you may want to allow ample time for questions and answers and keep everything else as short as possible.

Is this a trade event?

You may use this to refer to information about the marketplace, past, present and future size, developments, trends, opportunities, threats, coverage of likely trade actions and reactions, new trade policies, revised product standards, amended codes of good practice, or an acknowledgement of the success of key individuals and firms within the industry.

These subjects could be dealt with in various ways: through one or more speeches about different aspects of the trade and its marketplace, questions and answers, a discussion about forthcoming trade responses and policies and a presentation of awards to leading trade people and organizations.

Think about the order and length of each activity. Do you want speeches, discussions, presentations? Or speech, discussion, speech, discussion, presentations? Do you prefer short speeches and lengthier discussions with enough time set aside for the presentations to add prestige to them?

Is this a training event?

Topics to be covered at such an event might include: information about new laws and industry regulations; details of changing work practices; computerization; data about improved products and services, safety procedures, usage and maintenance. Anything else?

The best ways of covering these topics might be lectures about new laws followed by questions and answers from and to the floor; discussions about changing work practices; demonstrations of improved goods – perhaps followed by the opportunity to examine them.

This order might be the right one, or there could be a better one. Another possibility is many short sessions with breaks, to maintain interest and concentration. Do you want to allow plenty of time to lengthen sessions as required, to ask more questions, to attempt new practices under supervision, or to examine products until delegates are comfortable with them?

Are all the proposed business activities relevant?

Make sure that each session focuses on the key information you are trying to put over – detailed sales statistics, perhaps, or product specifications and other data, or possibly various tasks and duties which need to be carried out in a new way.

Design each session so that delegates can absorb the message in the easiest manner. A speech with sales statistics printed on simple-to-read charts, a presentation with data listed on handouts, or a physical demonstration of how a particular task should be done can help here.

Are these business activities interesting enough?

Be aware of how speakers will address the audience. If alone, can they handle it? If with aids, will they use visual ones such as flip-charts or overhead projectors, or audio-visual equipment such as slides with sound or videos?

Interest may wane if delegates are not given a chance to join in. Are there discussions, questions and answers and examinations – at frequent intervals?

Is the business programme relatively brief?

There is probably no ideal length for a conference – every one of them is different! It depends on what you are trying to put across, how you are going to put it over, and how quickly you want to do it. It should be long enough for you to convey your message and short enough to retain concentration and minimize costs. Achieving the right balance is difficult.

Is the business programme flexible?

Flexibility means having a programme which is easy to adjust at a later date, can be rearranged to make better use of speakers and which enables you to change the content, possibly by adding on sessions at the request of delegates. At the moment, you should simply have a framework to be amended and finalized nearer to the time.

Devising social activities

Mix business and pleasure together carefully at the conference. Too many speeches, facts, figures and so forth will tire delegates and they will soon become bored and disenchanted. Build some social activities into the event.

Have you thought about the provision of food and drink for speakers, delegates and their partners, as appropriate?

The type of catering provision you need to make depends on the type of conference and its overall timetable. The possibilities include a reception with non-alcoholic drinks and a finger buffet, coffee and tea breaks with light refreshments, lunches, buffets, sit-down meals and dinners. If laying on a dinner, do you want à la carte or table d'hôte, after-dinner speakers, a banquet or the full works – with entertainment too?

Decide on the order and length of meals and coffee or tea breaks. You could begin with a reception, serving coffee, tea and soft drinks, to allow people time to arrive, meet, relax, and socialize. After that you can have regular short breaks to break up the day. You may want to start with lunch, at midday or a little later, allowing enough time to relax but not so much that people relax completely! A dinner or a banquet at the end of the event will give people a chance to unwind, eat, drink and be merry.

What about partners while the business activities are taking place?

They may spend their time watching television or visiting the bar in the hotel and/or conference venue. Figure 3.1 below lists other pos-

☐ Abseiling
☐ Aerobics
☐ Archery

☐ Badminton
☐ Bars
☐ Basketball
☐ Bowls (carpet, grass)

☐ Cards (bridge, cribbage)
☐ Chess
☐ Computers
☐ Cricket
☐ Croquet
☐ Curling

☐ Dancing (ballroom, country, disco, rock-and-roll)

☐ Exhibitions

☐ Falconry
☐ Fancy dress
☐ Fishing (coarse, fly, lake)
☐ Football

☐ Gardens
☐ Golf
☐ Gymnasiums

☐ Hairdressers
☐ Health and beauty salons

☐ Jogging

☐ Netball
☐ Nightclubs

☐ Putting

☐ Quizzes

☐ Restaurants

☐ Saunas
☐ Shooting (clay pigeon, game, laser, pointball)
☐ Squash
☐ Swimming

☐ Television (satellite, terrestrial)
☐ Tennis (hard, soft, table)
☐ Treasure hunts

☐ Videos
☐ Volleyball

And many more

Figure 3.1   In-house entertainments: a checklist

☐	Abseiling	☐	Historic buildings
☐	Archery	☐	Hot air ballooning
☐	Art galleries		
		☐	Jogging
☐	Badminton		
☐	Ballet	☐	Leisure centres
☐	Bars		
☐	Basketball	☐	Mazes
☐	Beaches	☐	Model villages
☐	Bistros	☐	Museums
☐	Bowls (grass, ten-pin)		
☐	Bungee jumping	☐	Nature reserves
		☐	Netball
☐	Cafes	☐	Nightclubs
☐	Canals		
☐	Canoeing	☐	Obstacle courses
☐	Carnivals		
☐	Casinos	☐	Palaces
☐	Castles	☐	Parascending
☐	Cathedrals	☐	Parks (public, theme, wildlife)
☐	Caving	☐	Pubs
☐	Cinemas	☐	Putting
☐	Climbing (mountain, rock)		
☐	Concerts (classical, opera, rock)	☐	Racing (greyhound, horse, powerboat, saloon car, stock-car)
☐	Country parks		
☐	Cricket		
☐	Croquet	☐	Rafting
☐	Cruises (river, sea)	☐	Rambling
☐	Curling	☐	Restaurants
		☐	Riding (horse, pony)
☐	Dancing (ballroom, country, disco, rock-and-roll)	☐	Rugby (7-, 11-, 15-a-side)
☐	Driving (carriage, cars)	☐	Sailing
		☐	Saunas
☐	Exhibitions	☐	Scuba diving
		☐	Shooting (clay pigeon, game, laser, pointball)
☐	Falconry		
☐	Farms		
☐	Fishing (coarse, fly, lake, sea)	☐	Shopping
☐	Flying (helicopter, plane)	☐	Sightseeing
☐	Football (5-, 7-, 11-a-side)	☐	Skating (ice, roller)
☐	Funfairs	☐	Skiing (dry slope, water)
		☐	Snorkelling
☐	Gardens	☐	Squash
☐	Gliding (glider, hang, para-)	☐	Swimming
☐	Go-karting		
☐	Golf	☐	Tennis (hard, soft, table)
☐	Gymnasiums	☐	Train rides (steam)
		☐	Treasure hunts
☐	Hairdressers	☐	Trekking (pony)
☐	Health and beauty salons		

Figure 3.2   Outside entertainments: a checklist

☐ Volleyball	☐ War games
☐ Walking (flat, guided, hill, river-side, woods)	☐ Zoos
	And many more

Figure 3.2   Outside entertainments: a checklist (concluded)

sible in-house entertainments. Alternatively, they may be amused outside the hotel and/or conference venue by shopping or going to the theatre. Figure 3.2 on pages 26–27 lists further prospective outside entertainments. Some are interchangeable!

How should these entertainments be managed? Should partners be left alone to use a hotel's facilities as and when they want? Should you bring in entertainments for them, such as a fashion show or a clay pigeon shoot? Should they be encouraged to go out and about? To a garden show, perhaps? Alternatively, should you make the arrangements? A visit to a theme park, possibly?

When should these entertainments be arranged and for how long? Purely to coincide with business activities? Outside business hours too? For as long as partners want?

How about speakers, delegates and their partners outside the business activities?

They may want to be entertained inside or outside the hotel and/or conference venue. Refer to Figures 3.1 and 3.2 on pages 25–27 for lists of entertainments. They may not want to do anything if they have been working hard.

Any entertainments programme must be approached carefully. Most people will wish to be left alone. The rest of them may want you to arrange entertainments – can you arrange transport, schedules, book tickets and so on?

Think about when you should arrange entertainments and for how long. Should they be held before the conference begins so that people get to know each other, or during the event? Is this the most convenient time? If they take place after the event, the speakers, delegates and partners may not stay on. The social activities should last long enough to keep people happy but not be so lengthy that they interfere with business activities.

Are the social activities suited to participants?

Backgammon and chess may be too sedentary. Tennis and volleyball could be too lively. (Bungee jumping and hang-gliding are far too dangerous!) Take account of everyone's feelings. Remember that some people will want to participate part of the time, others occasionally and a proportion not at all.

Is the overall social programme complementary?

Consider whether it blends in well with the business programme and the theme, perhaps? If the theme is 'Becoming a Successful Seller' you could include competitive activities such as quizzes, an obstacle course or laser shooting. It should avoid intruding on the business programme though. The activities should be interesting but not so exciting that participants no longer concentrate on business matters, and energetic but not exhausting so that participants remain fresh and alert throughout the business activities.

Is the social programme flexible?

Can you change it nearer to the time, replace some activities on request, add to it if required or drop some activities if necessary? Can you make it flexible – perhaps to allow speakers and delegates to join in activities with their partners? At this stage, do you just have an outline of ideas to be adjusted and finalized at a later date?

Recommended reading

Burton, C. and Michael, N. (1992), *A Practical Guide to Project Management*, Kogan Page, London.
Haynes, M.E. (1990), *Project Management*, Kogan Page, London.

4

Planning a Schedule

Organizing a conference takes time. The smallest event with perhaps only 30 or so delegates may need three months to set up properly, while a larger one with hundreds of delegates in attendance can require as long as a year or even more. If you attempt to stage a conference too quickly it will probably be unsuccessful – and you will almost certainly be blamed for its failure. You need to calculate and then timetable your activities so that you have a realistic schedule which can be adhered to.

Calculating your activities

Try to list all the many and varied activities which are likely to comprise your workload up to, during and after the event. Attempt to take a broad view of the whole process. This will help you to encompass everything that needs to be done. Later on you can timetable the activities into a rather more formal schedule.

Have you set your objectives?

Who do you want to speak at and attend the conference? What type of event are you staging? What do you want speakers to say and delegates to do? When do you want to hold the event and when not? Where do you and the participants want the conference to be staged? Why are you organizing the event? How should the conference be carried out?

How long should it be? How does it fit into your overall marketing campaign?

Have you established your budget?

Have you listed the likely income from sponsors, delegates and so on? Detailed possible expenditure on venue hire, speakers' fees and so on? Compiled the budget, and confirmed sources of income and areas of expenditure? Composed the cashflow forecast showing income received, expenditure incurred, and when?

Have you drafted your programme?

Have you picked the right theme? Created business activities and decided on appropriate topics, the approach, order and length? Devised social activities, catering, partners' and participants' activities of a suitable content, approach, order and length?

Are you now planning your schedule *carefully*?

Have you identified all the key tasks and duties on a step-by-step basis? Worked out the correct order in which to do them?

What about choosing the venue? Overnight accommodation too?

Set criteria against which venues can be assessed, and select a location by conducting research or visiting towns and cities. Visit shortlisted venues and potential overnight accommodation. You can then make a provisional booking, attend to the paperwork, sign forms and, most importantly, keep everyone up to date with developments up to the event.

How about bringing in speakers?

Decide who are the right speakers for the particular event, how many you want and why. Know what qualities you are looking for and take account of influences on your choice. You may find speakers through internal sources or, very likely, through external ones. When you are commissioning speakers, first work out what will make them want to come along and then decide how to approach them in the most effective manner. Discuss what will be covered now and in the run-up to the event, and how you will keep in touch.

What about inviting delegates to the conference?

In picking suitable delegates, decide what type of person should attend and why. What factors should influence your selection, how many delegates should you invite, and why? Draw up a contacts list both from inside your organization and outside it. When approaching delegates, know why they will want to attend and invite them in the most appropriate manner. Give them the right information now and in the period leading to the conference. Stay in contact!

How about publicizing the event?

Issuing press releases   Before deciding whether or not to use press releases, understand their advantages and disadvantages, as well as how to write them and deploy them successfully.

Mailing letters   Recognize the pros and cons of direct mail and choose whether to use it or not. Be aware of how to compose mailshots and send them out properly.

Advertising in the press   Be conscious of the benefits and drawbacks of advertising in the press and decide whether it is suitable to your circumstances. Can you draft advertisements and place them effectively?

Are you employing outsiders at some stage?

Decide whether or not to commission outsiders and for what purpose. Weigh up the benefits and drawbacks. Look at the influences on your choice. You may need to share out the workload. Who can supply publicity material, transport people and goods, or decorate the venue? Who will provide equipment, facilities and services, maintain security, cater for the conference, arrange social activities and insure the event? If you are working with outside suppliers, identify the types of individuals and organizations you want to deal with, build up a contacts list and negotiate with them.

Are you speaking in public?

Assess your aims and objectives. Why are you speaking? Who is your audience and what do they want? For how long should you speak and how well does your speech fit into the overall programme? Where are you speaking?

When you are preparing to speak, sketch out a provisional framework for your speech noting the rough order and contents. Fill out the various points in the framework and make sure that you are building up a solid speech (draft notes to assist you).

Decide how and where to rehearse your speech – then do it! Check and amend key aspects and assess and adjust certain areas of your performance.

What about using equipment?

Decide whether to include visual aids – product displays, flip-charts and the like. Know their individual good and bad points and how to use them properly. Consider incorporating audio-visual aids – slides with sound, films and so on. Understand their particular positive and negative features and how to operate them successfully.

Make the most of any equipment used, recognizing the general benefits and drawbacks of employing aids. Decide which ones to use and be aware of the dos and don'ts of including equipment in the conference.

How about staging rehearsals?

Be well organized in coordinating everyone, getting speakers there and providing an audience. Are rehearsals taking place at the venue itself? Make sure suppliers do what they have agreed to do and check that the overnight accommodation is ready.

It may be up to you to supervise activities, ensuring the business programme unfolds satisfactorily, appraising the social programme, making certain the venue really is acceptable, and that the facilities, services and also the overnight accommodation are satisfactory .

Be aware of any last-minute changes that may be necessary, such as adjusting the business activities, changing the social activities, making amendments to the venue, adjustments to the facilities and services and changes to the overnight accommodation.

How about managing the event itself?

Ensure that everyone can get there – speakers and partners, delegates and partners. Check that all arrangements are finalized with the venue, the suppliers and for overnight accommodation.

Be in control of the business activities – speakers, topics included in the programme, the approach to each session and the order and length of the sessions. Perhaps you should also monitor the social activities – catering, partners' activities, speakers', delegates' and partners' activities. Make sure that the activities are approached in an appropriate manner, and that they are well ordered and of a suitable length. You are responsible for sending everyone home (speakers, delegates and their respective partners) and making sure everything is tidied up with the venue, suppliers and the overnight accommodation.

What about following through after the conference has ended?

Review the event – your initial plans, objective-setting, the budget and so on as well as the build-up, bringing in speakers, delegates and the like, the conference itself and the rehearsals, the business and social activities and so forth.

Consider writing a report highlighting the positive aspects of the event. Should you refer to the negative aspects too? Decide whether it was a success or failure and what you want to do differently next time.

Prepare for a possible future event by reading more widely, taking further advice, joining a trade body and going on training courses.

Timetabling your activities

Having composed a fairly lengthy list of activities that need to be carried out, you then have to arrange them into a timetable which you can follow up to and beyond the conference. Typically, you may be given six months to organize this event – obviously you will need to adjust your timetable accordingly if more or less time has been allocated.

What should be done in the first month?

- Take the decision to stage the event unless this is made by those above you in the organization.

- Appoint yourself as the conference organizer. Is any assistance available? (Probably not until the event begins!)
- Set your objectives: who, what, when, where, why and how.
- Establish the budget: calculate income and expenditure; draw up a budget and cashflow forecast form.
- Draft your programme: theme, business activities, social activities.
- Plan your schedule, including all of the key activities in an appropriate order.

The second month?

- Set criteria for selecting location of the conference, the venue and the overnight accommodation.
- Select the location. Conduct research, possibly travelling to towns and cities to make your choice.
- Choose the venue and overnight accommodation. Carry out simultaneous research, visiting potential sites and making the selection.
- Provisionally book the venue and the overnight accommodation. Deal with all the paperwork and forms.
- Decide on your speakers. What qualities are required and how many do you need?
- Find the speakers. Should they come from within your firm or from outside?
- Commission speakers. Tell them what they need to know and agree terms and so on.
- Amend the programme in the light of negotiations with speakers, if necessary. Some sessions may need to be longer, others shorter.
- Notify the venue and overnight accommodation of any changes: perhaps three smaller conference rooms are now required instead of the one large one originally booked, or double rather than single bedrooms if some partners will be attending.
- Check the budget and cashflow forecast to make sure all is in order.

How about the third month?

- Pick suitable delegates – who and how many.

- Draw up an internal and external contacts list.

- Approach delegates, putting over the correct information. Sort out paperwork and the like.

- Adjust the programme as a consequence of discussions with delegates, adding more sessions and different topics and adopting an alternative approach if required.

- Inform the venue, overnight accommodation and speakers about any adjustments – conference rooms being required for differing lengths of time, for example.

- Issue the first press releases to newspapers, magazines and other relevant media.

- Mail out the initial batch of letters to potentially interested individuals and perhaps to organizations as well.

- Advertise the conference in newspapers and magazines and anywhere else that is appropriate.

- Refer to your budget and cashflow forecast forms to ensure all is proceeding as planned.

In the fourth month?

- Commission any outsiders you may need to assist you – printers, mini-cab firms, designers, equipment suppliers, security personnel, caterers, entertainers, insurance companies.

- Share out the workload in supplying publicity material, transporting people and items, decorating the venue, maintaining security, catering, arranging social activities and insuring the conference.

- Identify who you want to work with and build a contacts list. Negotiate with them.

- Change the programme following dealings with outside suppliers if necessary. (Are the external social activities now planned?)

- Notify the venue, overnight accommodation, speakers and delegates of any changes.

- Mail out the second batch of letters to unresponsive individuals and organizations.

- Look at your budget and cashflow forecast again. Are they in line with expectations?

What should be done in the fifth month?

- Take an overview of what you have to do at the conference – your own input (speech or whatever).
- Prepare your speech. Draft a provisional framework and then fill out the points to build a solid speech.
- Rehearse your speech. Check and amend key aspects of it and assess and adjust your performance.
- Decide whether to use visual aids – but only if you can use them properly!
- If you decide to incorporate audio-visual aids, make sure that you can operate them successfully.
- Make the most of any equipment being used.
- Check the progress of outside suppliers (printers, mini-cab firms and so on).
- See that all is well with the venue, overnight accommodation, speakers and delegates, as appropriate.
- Mail out third and final batch of letters to stubbornly unresponsive individuals and organizations. Is it time to give up?
- Review the budget and cashflow forecast.

The sixth month?

- Coordinate everyone and everything for rehearsals – speakers, an appropriate audience, the venue, suppliers, overnight accommodation.
- Supervise the rehearsals, business and social programme. Check the venue, facilities and services and the overnight accommodation.
- Make any last-minute changes to the business activities, social activities, venue, facilities and services and overnight accommodation.
- Notify the venue, overnight accommodation, speakers, delegates and suppliers of these last-minute changes and double-check that they know.
- Issue the second batch of press releases to local newspapers, perhaps, and to magazines for review in their next issue.

– Check your budget and cashflow forecast forms for problems.

At the event and thereafter?

– Get everyone and everything well organized: speakers, delegates and partners, venue, suppliers, overnight accommodation.

– Watch the business programme, including the speakers, topics, approach, order and length.

– Monitor the social programme, checking on catering, partners' and all participants' activities, approach, order and length.

– Send everyone home: speakers, delegates and partners. Tidy everything up with the venue, suppliers and overnight accommodation.

– Review the event from setting objectives through to the conference itself. Ask speakers, delegates, partners, people at the venue, suppliers and managers of the overnight accommodation for their views.

– Write a report on strengths, weaknesses, conclusions and recommendations.

– Look to the future by reading more, taking advice and joining a trade body, perhaps. You might attend a training course – and start preparing for the next conference.

Recommended reading

Lehmkuhl, D. and Lamping, D. C. (1995), *Organising for the Creative Person*, Kogan Page, London.
Winston, S. (1994), *The Organised Executive*, Kogan Page, London.

5

Choosing the Venue

Be aware of the significance of staging your conference in a suitable place – the venue chosen can make or break your event. To choose the right venue you need to set your criteria, select a location and shortlist and visit venues before reaching your decision. Then you can make a provisional booking which will be amended and finalized at a later date.

Setting criteria

First draw up criteria against which different locations and venues can be measured and assessed. Thinking about the following questions should help you to compose your own particular mix of requirements.

What are your precise objectives and how will these influence your choice of venue?

Be aware of what those people coming to the conference want and expect from the location, venue and overnight accommodation. Can you afford to fulfil those needs and expectations? Can you afford not to?

How many are coming to the event and how much space do you need for them during the day and overnight? Consider the type of conference you are organizing. Is it an incentive event perhaps, which may be better suited to an exotic location or an unusual venue?

Are you giving delegates a detailed and informative message, full of facts and figures? Can you put over that type of message in an offbeat, distracting venue such as a ship? Is the timing of the conference going to limit your choice? An academic venue such as a university is unlikely to be available in term-time.

In which town or city should you stage the event and how far can it be held from head office? Check where speakers and delegates will be travelling from to see if there is a location which is convenient for everyone.

How will the conference be conducted? If one speaker will be addressing all the delegates, then one large room may suffice. Several speakers dealing with small groups of delegates may require numerous rooms. If there are social as well as business activities; are there other events and places to visit in the vicinity?

How much money do you have available to spend on the venue?

Do you have some for the basic hire charge at a fixed price or on a per capita basis? Enough for add-ons, facilities, services, equipment, technicians to assist, build-up charge, break-down charge? What type of venue and overnight accommodation can you afford – what are your financial limits?

How do your likely business and social activities fit together into your programme? How do they affect your choice of venue?

Is a particular town or city associated with your theme and promoting itself in a similar way? If so, you may be able to get together for your mutual benefit.

What are your proposed business activities? Would speeches and discussions about trading overseas be most suited to a location with international links? Might training sessions and demonstrations be ideally placed in a venue with the most modern, hi-tech equipment?

What are your planned social activities? If you are holding a reception, should you pick a town or city which has a tourist board that will stage one on your behalf? If you are holding a banquet, it is important that your selected venue can handle one successfully. Would a planned visit to a theme park limit your choice of location?

Selecting a location

With a clearer idea of what you want, you can move on to select the town or city where you will stage this conference. In all probability you will have already pencilled in perhaps three or four locations which seem to be suitably sited and now just need to make a firm choice. Various trade publications and bodies can provide helpful advice and information on this matter, as detailed in 'Reference Tools' and 'Useful Contacts', pages 215 and 219 respectively.

In particular, the British Association of Conference Towns (BACT) offers guidance and a free publication called the *British Conference Destinations Directory* which describes in some detail over a hundred leading conference towns. The *Conference Green Book* published by Benn Business Information Services Limited also supplies data about prospective conference locations. Figures 5.1 and 5.2 on pages 42 and 44 contain examples of the information provided by those publications.

When studying readily available material and subsequently visiting towns and cities on your shortlist, address these specific issues before reaching that all-important decision.

Is the town or city attractive to everyone?

Will speakers want to come along, and will delegates feel excited enough to want to attend?

Is it convenient for everyone?

Are road, rail, sea and air links satisfactory (as appropriate)? Will participants be able to reach the location on time and in a relaxed mood, or will you have to delay the start of the event (not a good idea)? Will they be able to arrive home at a reasonable hour? Will you have to cut short the conference (an equally bad idea)?

Is there sufficient public transport in and around the town or city?

Are there buses for partners to use during the day and for speakers, delegates and partners in the evenings? Can taxis be hired quickly and easily, or retained for participants' use only? Should you hire bicycles for health-conscious speakers, delegates and partners?

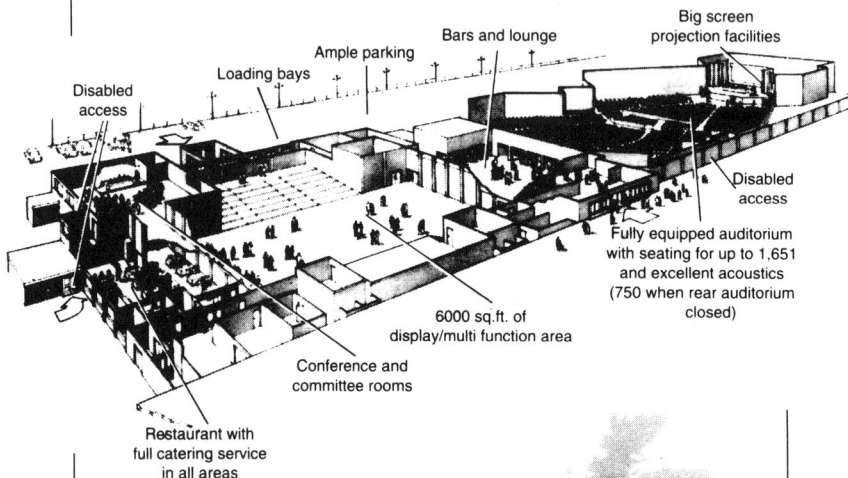

Figure 5.1   Extract, *British Conference Destinations Directory*

SOUTHPORT

Combine a first class conference service, a wealth of specialist conference facilities and an elegant Victorian resort and you have Southport.

Perfectly located on the North West of England's picturesque coastline, the town offers easy access to all modes of transportation and has the unique feature of 'walkability' as all the town's excellent facilities are within a short flat walk of each other.

Southport Theatre and Floral Hall Complex is designed to accept a multi conference facility including exhibitions, product launches and training seminars, as well as serious political arenas.

With a large parking area at the rear, loading and unloading are easy. Cars, boats and articulated trucks can all be accommodated at the Complex.

Professionalism and care are the key elements of the in-house catering service available at the Complex. A complete multi-functional catering operation is available to suit all budgets and tastes.

Excellent Accommodation is available in Southport ranging from family run guesthouses through to premier four star venues. The town's hoteliers are most appreciative of the needs of delegates and are always amenable to fit in with the conference schedule for meals, receptions etc.. As a resort is able to offer such a wide range of accommodation, prices are reflected accordingly, so there is always something to suit your conference.

Many of the hotels are able to offer excellent in-house conference facilities, therefore ensuring that the event is self-contained.

Entertainment and Relaxation are vital to the success of a conference and Southport offers a wide range of facilities for both.

Partner packages can also be arranged through the Conference Office.

One Call Does It All so make your conference special and telephone today.

CONTACT
Maxine Bowes
Conference Officer
Sefton MBC Tourism &
Attractions Dept
PO Box 25 Promenade
Southport PR9 0DZ
Tel: 0151 934 2402
Fax: 0151 934 2418

Access
AIR: Manchester Ringway 45 miles
RAIL: Southport
ROAD: M58/A565

Conference Venue Capacity
Max. seating of major conference venue 1651

Accommodation
950 hotel/venue bedrooms with ensuite facilities
2000 hotel/venue bedrooms within 1 mile radius of main venue
2050 hotel/venue bedrooms within 5 mile radius of main venue

Exhibition Capacity
Max. exhibition space 757 sq m in one venue

Services
* Venue advice/selection
* Accommodation booking
* Delegate information
* Preparation of bid documents & presentation
* Advice on access & local transport
* Advice on tours/social programmes
* Familiarisation visits
* Advice on local support services

View of Lord Street

Figure 5.1 Extract, *British Conference Destinations Directory* (concluded)

Weybridge

Oatlands Park Hotel
Weybridge

Oatlands Park Hotel
146 Oatlands Drive, Weybridge
Surrey KT13 9HB
England
Tel: (0932) 847242 Telex:
915123
Fax: (0932) 842252

General Manager:
Stephen Craner
Conference Contact:
Barbara Dadoush

MIA
MEMBER

Oatlands Park has been operating as a hotel since 1856 although originally built as a country house in 1794 in the Gothic style of that period, after a fire destroyed the previous building dating back to 1689. Set in acres of peaceful secluded grounds it is the ideal setting for a working session followed by relaxation.

The 117 bedrooms comprise superior and deluxe rooms. All are equipped with radio, satellite TV, direct dial telephone, tea/coffee making facilities and hairdryers.

Private dining can be arranged in the York Suite, Drawing Room and Garden Room which seat 220, 60 and 20 respectively. Alternatively a creative a la carte menu is served in the Broadwater Restaurant which seats up to 200. There is also a comfortable lounge bar which opens onto the patio.

How to get there

Oatlands Park is perfectly situated for all major travel links, with London being only a 25 minute train journey away and the nearby orbital motorway, the M25 ensuring easy access to Heathrow, Gatwick and all parts of the UK.

Meeting Facilities

The York Suite is the main conference room at Oatlands Park, seating up to 300 theatre style or 220 for a banquet. This divides into two separate rooms each seating 200 and 70 theatre style.

The Drawing Room and Garden Room are ideally suited to smaller events seating up to a maximum of 70 people. There are also two Boardrooms, the Surrey and Cedar Rooms, available seating up to 20 each. Six syndicate rooms are also available

For a minimum of 10 delegates a competitively priced inclusive conference package is available.

All rooms benefit from natural daylight and have blackout facilities.

For further technical details of the Meeting Rooms please see the Conference Blue Book.

Sports and Leisure Facilities

On Site

Tennis facilities are available on site and themed evenings can be arranged.

Other facilities includes laser clay shooting, archery and rifle shooting.

Other Facilities Nearby

Delegates at Oatlands Park can enjoy the excellent facilities of several local golf courses including Foxhills Country Club, Silvermere and St. Georges, Weybridge. The famous courses at Wentworth, Sunningdale and Royal Berkshire are also within easy reach.

Arrangements can be made for hotel guests to use the leisure facilities at a nearby Country Club. These include tennis, squash, indoor swimming pool, gym and golf.

Permits can be obtained for guests to fish either the Thames or the Wey just a mile from the hotel.
Horse riding can be arranged at a nearby stables and prices are available on

application to reception.

Laser clay pigeon shooting, archery and rifle shooting are available in the grounds on request.

Special Features

Situated just 5 miles from Hampton Court, Oatlands Park has many historic connections with Henry VIII and other royalty. The hotel was built on the site of a hunting lodge on the estate where the palace was built for his wife Anne of Cleves and it is rumoured that he secretly married his next queen, Katherine Howard, in the chapel.

Charles I made his home at Oatlands and a fine cedar tree, said to have been planted in commemoration of the birth of his son, Prince Henry, still stands beside the main drive.

In 1790 Oatlands was home to the Duke and Duchess of York and some of the headstones from the Duchess' dog cemetery can be seen set into the lawn by the Broadwater Restaurant.

Delegates at Oatlands can enjoy the hotels beautiful grounds and a relaxing walk around the Broadwater Lake.

Oatlands Park is the ideal setting for a Tudor Banquet with a mock up of Henry VIII's royal court or many other themed evenings. There is a varied programme of live music every Sunday lunchtime.

The Honeymoon Suite features a magnificent four poster bed.

On Site

Tennis

Rural Setting

Entertainments

Helipad

Laser Clay Pigeon Shooting

Archery

Rifle Shooting

Nearby

Golf

Swimming

Squash

Leisure Complex

Fishing

Horse Riding

Figure 5.2   Extract, *Conference Green Book*

What is there to do in and around the town or city?

Are there shops to look at, gardens to visit, trips to enjoy and so on for partners who have free time while the business programme is being conducted? Are there pubs, restaurants, theatres, nightclubs, and such like for speakers and delegates when business activities have been concluded?

What other events are being held there at the same time?

These may be useful for keeping partners occupied during the business programme although they could also be a distraction, competing with your conference for attention. Think carefully!

Does the town or city try to attract conferences?

Is there a tourist board to help and advise you? If so, can it offer general advice, recommend venues and overnight accommodation, comment constructively on your proposed programme, suggest social activities for your participants or anything else? If not, can anyone else offer you assistance of any kind? A convention bureau might be able to provide general guidance, help to stage a reception, supply promotional literature when you want to publicize the event, mail out literature such as 'What's On' guides to participants and possibly give other help as well.

Of the utmost importance, does the town or city provide a good choice of conference and overnight accommodation?

Is there a sufficient number of conference venues in the locality for you to choose from? Do these venues meet your set criteria? For overnight accommodation, check that there is a choice of hotels for you to pick from which meet your requirements.

Shortlisting venues

Having selected the right location, you can press ahead to shortlist conference venues and overnight accommodation as relevant. Once again, numerous trade associations and publications can be of assistance to

VENUE LOCATION SERVICE

I have the following meeting/conference requirements

Name: _____ Position: _____

Organisation: _____

Address: _____

_____ Postcode: _____

Telephone: _____ Fax: _____

Type & length of event: _____

Proposed date(s): _____ No. of delegates: _____

Type of venue: _____ Accommodation? YES/NO

Style of seating: _____ Syndicate rooms: _____

AV equipment: _____ Budget: £ _____

Preferred location(s): _____

Please arrange for me to receive information from the following BACT members:

☐ Aberdeen	☐ Calderdale	☐ Essex	☐ Lake District (South)	☐ Norwich	☐ Surrey
☐ Arfon	☐ Cambridge	☐ Exeter	☐ Lancaster	☐ Nottingham	☐ Swansea
☐ Ayrshire	☐ Canterbury	☐ Gloucester	☐ Leeds	☐ Perthshire	☐ Swindon
☐ Basingstoke	☐ Cardiff	☐ Grantham & Stamford	☐ Leicestershire	☐ Peterborough	☐ Taunton
☐ Bath	☐ Carlisle	☐ Great Yarmouth	☐ Lincoln	☐ Plymouth	☐ Teignbridge
☐ Bedford	☐ Cheltenham Spa	☐ Greater Glasgow	☐ Llandudno	☐ Poole	☐ Telford & Shropshire
☐ Belfast	☐ Chester & Cheshire	☐ Greater Manchester	☐ London	☐ Portsmouth	☐ Tenby
☐ Birmingham	☐ Chippenham	☐ Guernsey	☐ Luton	☐ Preston	☐ Wakefield
☐ Black Country	☐ Clwyd	☐ Harrogate	☐ Malvern	☐ Radnorshire	☐ Weston Super Mare
☐ Blackpool	☐ Cotswolds	☐ Hastings	☐ Manchester/Trafford	☐ Reading	☐ West Wiltshire
☐ Bolton	☐ Coventry	☐ Hull	☐ Merseyside	☐ Scarborough	☐ Weymouth/Portland
☐ Bournemouth	☐ Derby	☐ Inverness	☐ Middlesbrough	☐ Sheffield	☐ Winchester
☐ Bradford	☐ Doncaster	☐ Ipswich	☐ Milton Keynes	☐ Skegness	☐ Windsor
☐ Brecon	☐ Dundee	☐ Isle of Man	☐ Morecambe	☐ Southend-on-Sea	☐ Worthing
☐ Bridlington	☐ Durham	☐ Isle of Wight	☐ Newcastle Upon Tyne	☐ South Glamorgan	☐ Wrexham
☐ Brighton	☐ Eastbourne	☐ Jersey	☐ Newport	☐ Southport	
☐ Bristol	☐ Edinburgh	☐ Kent's Leisure Coast	☐ Northamptonshire	☐ Stafford	
☐ Buxton	☐ English Riviera	☐ Kirklees	☐ North Devon	☐ Suffolk Coast	

NAME: _____ TITLE: _____

ORGANISATION: _____

ADDRESS: _____

_____ POSTCODE: _____

TELEPHONE: _____ EXT: _____

Figure 5.3   Venue location form

Leeds

Leeds Hilton
Leeds

Leeds Hilton
Neville Street, Leeds
West Yorkshire LS1 4BX
Tel: (0532) 442000 Telex: 557143
Fax: (0532) 433577

Hilton National

General Manager: **Chris Allcoat**
Conference Contact: **Kathy Whitehead**

HILTON
LEEDS CITY

A modern purpose built hotel situated in the centre of the city. It is located adjacent to Leeds railway station, 8 miles from Leeds/Bradford Airport and 1/4 mile from the M1/M62 motorways.

There is a total of 206 bedrooms comprising 23 Plaza Rooms, 87 doubles, 93 twins and 1 disabled room all with ensuite bathrooms. All rooms are equipped with radio, colour T.V., direct dial telephone and tea/coffee making facilities.

The Seasons Restaurant, located on the Reception level serves the discerning guest a seasonal menu with many regional dishes, or a buffet featuring the Hors d'oeuvrie. A brasserie style menu is also available all day, in the adjacent Blue Notes Bar. This bar offers a sophisticated and relaxing place to have a drink after a busy day.

The Hotel's meeting facilities comprise of the Brigantes Suite which can accommodate up to 400 delegates theatre style, with 6 further conference rooms accommodating from 10 to 60 delegates. The hotel offers a fully equipped Business and Meeting Service Centre to provide full secretarial support.

How to get there

The hotel is within walking distance of Leeds Central Railway Station, 10 miles from Leeds/Bradford Airport, 3/4 mile from M1/M621 and M62. Car Parking for 80 approx.

Daily Delegate Rate - £35.00
24 Hr Delegate Rate: £135.00

MEETING ROOM INFORMATION

ROOM NAME	Brigantes	Neville	Danby	Thoresby	Kitson	Ingram	Beckett
FLOOR	3	4	4	4	4	4	4
CAPACITIES							
theatre	400	150	60	30	30	24	-
classroom	180	80	30	14	14	12	-
boardroom	-	-	25	16	16	12	12
U-shape	-	-	25	16	16	12	12
lunch/dinner	300	150	30	16	16	12	12
reception	500	200	50	40	30	20	-
DIMENSIONS							
length							
feet	66'8"	48'	40'	27'3"	20'8"	19'2"	20'
(metres)	(20.3)	(14.6)	(12.6)	(8.3)	(6.4)	(5.9)	(6.3)
width							
feet	45'6"	40'	18'	16'	18'	16'	16'
(metres)	(14)	(12.4)	(5.5)	(4)	(5.5)	(4.9)	(4.9)
area							
sq ft	3033	1948	720	436	372	306	320
(sq.m)	(284)	(181)	(63)	(40.7)	(35.2)	(29)	(30)
height (maxima)							
feet	11'6"	10'6"	9'	9'	9'	9'	9'
(metres)	(3.51)	(3.2)	(2.74)	(2.74)	(2.74)	(2.74)	(2.74)
height (minima)							
feet	9'8"	10'6"	9'	9'	9'	9'	9'
(metres)	(2.94)	(3.2)	(2.74)	(2.74)	(2.74)	(2.74)	(2.74)

TECHNICAL INFORMATION

	Brigantes	Neville	Danby	Thoresby	Kitson	Ingram	Beckett
LIGHTING							
tungsten/fluorescent	tungsten	both	both	both	both	both	both
controls in room	yes	yes	yes	yes	yes	yes	yes
dimmers	yes	yes	yes	yes	yes	yes	yes
black out	yes	yes	yes	yes	yes	yes	yes
windows	no	yes	yes	yes	yes	yes	yes
SOUND							
sound system fitted	yes	yes	no	yes	yes	yes	yes
POWER							
no. of 13 amp sockets	11	11	6	4	4	4	4
3 -phase available	yes	no	no	no	no	no	no
ACCESS							
door height							
feet	7'	6'6"	8'	8'	8'	8'	6'
(metres)	(2.14)	(2)	(2.4)	(2.4)	(2.4)	(2.4)	(2.4)
door width							
feet	6'6"	5'	4'	4'	4'	4'	4'
(metres)	(2)	(1.5)	(1.2)	(1.2)	(21.2)	(1.2)	(1.2)
MISCELLANEOUS							
telephone points	yes	yes	yes	yes	yes	yes	yes
air conditioning	yes	yes	yes	yes	yes	yes	yes

CONFERENCE EQUIPMENT: *PA system, Radio microphone, Hand Held microphone, Built in Back Projection set consisting of a 35ml projector, TV & Video, 5 x OHP, 3 x 35ml projectors, 5 x 6' x 6' screens, 8 flipchart stands.*

208

Figure 5.4 Extract, *Conference Blue Book*

you at this stage. Most notably, the British Association of Conference Towns (BACT), the tourist boards of most towns and cities and some organizations belonging to the Association of Conference Executives (ACE) and the Meetings Industry Association (MIA) provide a free, venue location service whereby you supply them with your requirements which are then matched to potentially suitable venues on your behalf. Figure 5.3 on page 46 is an example of the type of form you will need to complete.

If you prefer to take a do-it-yourself approach, Benn's *Conference Blue Book* covers nearly 5,000 venues across the British Isles and lists the key technical information you need to know in order to compose a shortlist. Refer to Figure 5.4 on page 47 for an example of the information given in this publication. Should you subsequently contact venues, they will send you a preliminary information pack similar to the one reproduced as Figure 5.5 on pages 49 to 63. If a venue is worth scheduling for a visit you must be able to answer the following questions in a positive manner:

Is the venue easy to find and readily accessible?

Can it be reached on foot, perhaps from the nearest railway station, or by car, using a map and/or referring to signposts? Are there satisfactory public transport links to and from the site?

Is it the right size for your needs?

Can all the delegates be accommodated, with everybody in one room for some sessions and separated into several, smaller groups on other occasions? Are you sure you can fit in a stage, equipment, product displays and delegates comfortably? Is there easy access for delegates – including disabled ones? Is it easy to manœuvre and display equipment?

Does the venue offer everything you need to run a successful conference?

Do the facilities include an induction loop, toilets for disabled speakers, delegates and partners, soundproofed rooms and anything else you need?

Are there photocopiers, fax machines, secretarial and translation services? Are flip-charts, slide projectors and screens and video machines

SWANSEA INSTITUTE OF HIGHER EDUCATION

ATHROFA ABERTAWE

CONFERENCE / VACATION COURSE FACILITIES

Figure 5.5 Venue information pack

CONFERENCE FACILITIES

THE INSTITUTE - OUR LOCATION

Swansea Institute of Higher Education has a reputation internationally for its friendly, welcoming environment for students, staff and visitors. It is now developing into an attractive Conference Centre where all Organisations can take full advantage of first-class residential and teaching accommodation as well as facilities for social functions at reasonable cost.

There are two main campuses within a radius of two miles:

TOWNHILL Campus located high above the City of Swansea. Enjoys breathtaking views of Swansea Bay and neighbouring Mumbles.

MOUNT PLEASANT Campus which is located near Swansea City Centre, is non-residential but offers other facilities similar to those at the Townhill Campus.

RESIDENTIAL ACCOMMODATION

We offer residential facilities for up to 250 guests in three modern Halls of Residence which are all located on the Townhill Campus about two miles from the City Centre. The Halls have single rooms with fitted wardrobe and hand washbasin, 13 amp power point; showers, toilets, bathrooms and a Launderette. There are kitchens on each floor providing limited facilities for light snacks and refreshments.

(Note - We regret that we do not provide facilities for very young children.)

CATERING

Our Catering Department offers a full range of services to suit all tastes. In addition to a variety of main meals throughout the day, morning coffee, afternoon tea, and packed lunches for day visits can also be provided at reasonable prices.

Meal times are normally:-

BREAKFAST from 8.00 am to 9.00 am

LUNCH from 12 noon to 1.30 pm

EVENING MEAL from 5.30 pm to 6.30 pm

Drinks vending machines are situated at various locations on the campuses.

Wines, beers and soft drinks are available during main meal times. Wine and Sherry receptions can also be arranged on request.

We have facilities for receptions, buffets, and parties. Dinner-Dances can also be catered for at Townhill. Bookings should be arranged with the Conference Officer.

Figure 5.5 Venue information pack (continued)

CONFERENCE FACILITIES

LEISURE AND RECREATION

Swansea Institute of Higher Education is fortunate to be at the centre of a thriving Tourist and Leisure Industry enjoying all the benefits this provides.

On Campus (at Townhill)

The gym is available for Badminton, Netball and indoor recreational and physical training. Badminton may also be played in the Main Hall when not in use for other activities.

Bar facilities available if booked in advance with the Conference Officer.

Off Campus

Swansea has a great deal to offer the sports enthusiast.

The Swansea Leisure Centre, applauded as one of the top twenty attractions in the UK, offers Swimming, Squash, Badminton, Bowls, Bowling, Powerhouse, Table Tennis, Sauna, Solarium and many other activities.

The Morfa Stadium, on the fringe of the city, is an excellent modern athletics stadium. Its facilities include an Indoor Tennis centre, All-Weather Surface pitches and a Dry Ski Slope.

Other Leisure and Recreation activities in Swansea, Mumbles and Gower include:

Watersports

(Swimming, sailing, surfing, wind surfing, water skiing and sub-aqua diving).

Climbing on challenging cliffs in and around Gower.

Horse Riding and Pony Trekking

Cycling. Cycle hire is available. Tracks are laid through rural areas and along the seafront.

Golf

Parachuting, Gliding, Hang-gliding and Microlighting

Recreation and Leisure activities for all.

Figure 5.5 Venue information pack (continued)

SOCIAL AND OTHER ACTIVITIES

Swansea is a busy shopping and entertainment centre with an active cultural life in which the Theatre plays an important part. A full programme of varied Plays, Musicals and other entertainment as well as a season of Opera and Ballet are all on offer at the Grand in Central Swansea, The Dylan Thomas in the Maritime Quarter and the Taliesin on the University College campus.

For other branches of the Arts the Glynn Vivian Art Gallery has frequent displays and specialist exhibitions of international repute.

The British Institution and Swansea Industrial and Maritime Museums (near the Maritime Quarter) are also centres of cultural interest well worth a visit.

So, on or off campus, there is plenty to do while you are at Swansea Institute.

Figure 5.5   Venue information pack (continued)

ROUTES

LOCATION

Sketch maps of Swansea and the location of the Institute are shown overleaf.

Arriving by Air

From Heathrow Airport. Ask for directions at the Heathrow
Central Bus Station which is the National Express Service terminus.   The national coaches
(Number 506) run approximately 2 hourly direct to Swansea.   Refreshments available on the
coach* From Gatwick Airport:

(i)   South Terminal. From Stand 625 at Central Bus Station.

(ii)   North Terminal. From Stand 625 in the Lower Forecourt.

The 625 Service runs either direct to Swansea or you will change at Cardiff and take the hourly
'bus shuttle' to Swansea.*

*From Swansea Coach Station take a taxi to the Institute.

Arriving by Car

Via Cardiff and Port Talbot

The M4 motorway is only three miles from Swansea City Centre and, with the M5 link, provides
fast motoring from London, the Midlands, North and South East England and the West
Country. At the end of the M4 (Port Talbot) continue on the A48 (dual carriageway), across
the River Tawe bridge and turn left on A483 to Swansea.

For Mount Pleasant, Alexandra Road and Penybryn: turn right at the Swansea Leisure Centre
traffic lights and travel along Princess Way; and half way around the Kingsway Roundabout and
straight ahead; then follow the Institute signs.

For Townhill: From Cardiff and Southern parts of England continue passed the Swansea
Leisure Centre and County Hall along the sea front, passing the University College, then turn
right on A4216 along Sketty Lane; follow the signpost for Carmarthen to Sketty Cross Traffic
Lights, proceed through the traffic lights to the second mini roundabout (Broadway) bear left
over zebra crossing and turn right at mini roundabout into Townhill Road.

Figure 5.5   Venue information pack (continued)

From West Wales via Carmarthen

Leave the M4 at junction 47 and follow A4216 until right turn into Cockett Road (signposted Mumbles and Sketty). Continue through traffic lights until sharp left at mini roundabout at Broadway for Townhill Road.

Arriving by Train

Alexandra Road is 5 minutes walk from the British Rail Station. Mount Pleasant and Penybryn 10 minutes - but on a steep hill, so allow extra time if carrying luggage. For Townhill take No. 12 or 13 bus at Orchard Street for Graiglwyd Square.

Arriving by Bus

National Coaches arrive at the Quadrant Bus Station. Alexandra Road is 10 minutes walk - or take No. 12 or 13 bus to Orchard Street. For Mount Pleasant and Penybryn: No. 12 or 13 bus to Mount Pleasant. For Townhill: No. 12 or 13 bus to Graiglwyd Square (approximately every 15 minutes) and walk down hill along Townhill Road. Note: No. 43 bus also passes the Townhill Campus but takes about 30 minutes and does not run after 5.15 pm.

(By prior arrangement with the Conference Officer at the Institute , the College Minibus can meet visitors at the Swansea Railway and Coach Stations.)

Figure 5.5   Venue information pack (continued)

TARIFF AND DATES OF AVAILABILITY

Accommodation is available during the Institute vacation periods. The relevant dates for the forthcoming year are as follows:-

SUMMER   Monday 27 June 1994   Friday 23rd September 1994

CHRISTMAS Monday 19 December 1994   Friday 6 January 1995

EASTER   Monday 10 April 1995   Friday 28 April 1995

Please check these dates before booking. Bookings are not available for Christmas Day, Boxing Day and New Year's Day. In addition, some rooms may be available during term-time.   For further information please telephone the Conference Officer on Swansea (0792) 481208

TARIFF
(Subject to Annual Review)

RESIDENCE AND CATERING

Residential accommodation per night	14.00
Breakfast	2.60
Lunch	3.15
Dinner	4.25
Full Board Res. Acc. daily charge	24.00
Tea and Coffee	0.75
Packed Lunch	2.60

Current prices could be increased, and these will be notified.

Any special requirements for meals should be made directly with the College Caterers.

NON-RESIDENTIAL ACCOMMODATION

Per session (3 hours) 9.00 - 12.00 noon, 1.00 - 4.00 pm, 6.00 - 9.00 pm.

	£
Assembly/Dining Hall	31.00
Lecture Theatre	31.00
Conference Room	31.00
Gymnasium	31.00
Common Room	21.00
Lecture Room	21.00
Laboratory	21.00

Figure 5.5   Venue information pack (continued)

DAILY USE RATE

CCTV	31.00
OHP	15.00
Film Projector	21.00
Piano	10.00

OTHER RATES

Photocopies:	Per single copy	0.10
	Per 15 copies	1.00
	Per 20 copies	1.50
	Per 30 copies	2.00
Minibus (daily hire)		22.00
Van (daily hire)		15.00
Fuel Charge per mile		0.28

ABOVE CHARGES ARE SUBJECT OT VAT

Figure 5.5   Venue information pack (continued)

SWANSEA INSTITUTE OF HIGHER EDUCATION

APPLICATION FOR CONFERENCE FACILITIES

Name of Organisation _____

Local Organiser _____

Address for Correspondence _____

_____

Tel No: _____ Fax No: _____

Dates required from _____ to _____

Purpose for which accommodation is to be reserved (i.e. Meetings, Conference, Course, Seminar etc.)

_____

Campus: MOUNT PLEASANT / TOWNHILL / ALEXANDRA ROAD

Anticipated Arrival Time _____ Departure Time _____

Total Number of Sessions for room use

9 am	-	12 noon _____
1 pm	-	4 pm _____
6 pm	-	9 pm _____

Total Number of Sessions _____

Accommodation required: FULL BOARD / BED AND BREAKFAST / ROOMS ONLY

Residential Accommodation and Facilities required:

	Number of Rooms	Number of Rooms	Additional Facilities
	Males	Females	Conference Room Lecture Room Common Room Assembly Room Lecture Theatre Gymnasium Laboratory AVA Photocopier Car Parking Telephone
Study / Bedrooms) Staff) Accommodation)			
GRAND TOTAL			TOTAL

NB   **No reduction will be made if accommodation is cancelled within 7 days of booking dates. All accommodation reserved will be charged for and no reduction will be made for accommodation not used.**

Figure 5.5   Venue information pack (continued)

CONFERENCE FACILITIES

CONDITIONS OF HIRE

AGE LIMIT

The Institute does not normally accept reservations from groups whose members are under 16 years of age. The Conference Officer should be contacted with any special requests.

ACCOMMODATION

The various types of accommodation are as listed in the Booking Form but the Institute reserves the right to vary the allocation of accommodation.

DAMAGE

The Organiser of the Visit/Conference/Course/Seminar etc, will be held responsible for making good any damage to Institute property in accordance with the terms of the Indemnity included in the Application Form and the Organisation must meet the cost of making good any damage incurred.

ACCIDENTS

All accidents which take place on Institute premises must be reported to the Conference Officer or to the Campus Main Reception during normal office hours or the Halls Office (Security Staff) after normal hours.

FIRE REGULATIONS

Limits on the numbers which can be accommodated in Lecture Theatres, Halls and Lecturing Rooms are specified by the Fire Officer and must not be exceeded. Details available from the Conference Officer.

Fire Notices are distributed in all main areas and must be observed.

FREEDOM OF SPEECH

The Organiser must also agree to Indemnify the Institute against any damage or expense or other claims arising from any breach of the Institute's policy relating to Freedom of Speech legislation.

LIABILITY

The Institute does not accept responsibility for loss or damage to property brought on to the Institute's premises, including personal property. The Institute must be indemnified by the Organisation against any claims by any of its members in respect of injury to persons and loss or damage to property or persons which arise directly or indirectly from use of Institute premises.

Figure 5.5   Venue information pack (continued)

BOOKING AND CANCELLATION PROCEDURES

Booking

The Conference Officer will confirm whether the dates requested are available. Bookings should be made by completing and returning the forms in this Brochure to the Institute.

Booking Fees

A 10% Booking Fee is required which is calculated on the anticipated total charge. A cheque for this fee, made payable to Swansea Institute of Higher Education, should be enclosed with the Booking Form.

Confirmation

Confirmation in writing will be sent on receipt of your completed application and Booking Fee.

Cancellation Charges

No reduction will be made if accommodation is cancelled within 7 days of booking dates. All accommodation reserved will be charged for and no reduction will be made for accommodation not used.

Payment

All charges must be paid in full within 30 days of the date of Invoicing. If Invoice is not settled within this period, the Institute reserves the right to impose a surcharge at the prevailing bank interest rate.

<u>ACCEPTANCE</u>

I understand, accept and agree to abide by all the procedures, terms and conditions contained herein.

Signature _____
Conference Organiser

Date _____

Name of Organisation _____

Address _____

_____

Telephone Number _____

Fax Number _____

Figure 5.5 Venue information pack (continued)

CONFERENCE FACILITIES

GENERAL INFORMATION

We have several lecture rooms, classrooms, workshops fully equipped laboratories etc. and facilities suitable for conferences, courses, seminars and social functions which include:

TOWNHILL CAMPUS

Main Hall, situated in the Centre of the Campus which seats approximately 350. It has a large curtained stage leading to changing rooms.

Gymnasium, situated next to the Main Hall

Lecture Theatre, which is equipped with Film Projector and other AVA facilities and has fixed seating for over 150 and features a control lectern.

Conference Room, which can accommodate approximately 40-50, located on the top floor of the Library Block with magnificent panoramic view of Swansea Bay and Mumbles Head.

Senior Common Room, which is an attractive functional room and is ideally suited for small working groups or informal functions.

MOUNT PLEASANT AND TOWNHILL CAMPUSES

There are numerous Lecture Rooms, Committee Rooms, Common Rooms and Lecture Theatres which can all be used in conjunction with one or more of the larger rooms for group discussions and meetings, hired separately.

SAFETY

Please read carefully the Fire Notices displayed on Campus. Fire Drills are held regularly in the main teaching areas, Halls of Residence, and other non-residential areas. All persons on Campus must comply with evacuation procedures. Under no circumstances should fire alarms and Fire Safety Notices be ignored or tampered with.

SECURITY

There are security patrols throughout the night for Halls of Residence and an alarm system in operation. Resident guests and visitors are responsible for their own personal belongings. The Institute cannot accept responsibility for any article lost of stolen. For personal items of value, special arrangements may be made for their safe deposit upon request to the Conference Officer.

Figure 5.5   Venue information pack (continued)

CAR PARKING

There is limited parking available on the Mount Pleasant Campus, but at the Townhill Campus there is ample car parking during vacations. Car parking arrangements must be agreed with the Conference Officer before the arrival date for visitors.

TELEPHONES

There are card and coin-operated pay-phones in various locations around the Institute and in Halls of Residence.

TRANSPORT

The College Minibus is available for transporting visitors to and from the public service transport stations e.g. Railway and Bus, subject to advance booking with the Conference Officer.

POSTAL SERVICES

Post is delivered twice daily on weekdays. Mail for resident visitors may be collected from the Townhill Reception desk between 8.30.am and 4.30 pm and on Saturday mornings by prior arrangement with Security Staff. All mail for residential courses should be addressed by individual name and course or conference etc to Swansea Institute of Higher Education, Townhill Road, Swansea SA2 OUT.

LAUNDERETTE

The launderette is located on the Ground Floor of the Dyfed Hall which is open from 9.00 am to 9.00 pm each day. This is a coin operated system using 20p coins.

ROOM KEYS

Room keys for residential courses should be collected by the Course Organiser from the Halls Office at Townhill on arrival. A charge will be made for replacement of lost keys.

MEDICAL FACILITIES

The Institute has an 'on call' Medical Officer. There is a local hospital nearby. Conference Organisers may wish to bring a Nurse from their own Organisation which is permitted by prior agreement with the Conference officer

BAR

There is a fully licensed Bar on the Townhill Campus, and a licensed Restaurant on the Mount Pleasant campus, both of which can be booked during vacations by prior arrangement with the Conference Officer. Special licences or extensions of the permitted licensing hours for special functions can be arranged but such requests must be made to the Conference Officer at least four weeks prior to Conference. A special licence fee is normally payable.

Figure 5.5 Venue information pack (continued)

TO ALL VISITORS

There is a welcome awaiting all visitors to Swansea Institute of Higher Education.

CROESO i ATHROFA ABERTAWE

We hope your stay is a most enjoyable one.

GERALD STOCKDALE   ALBERT GARDNER
Principal   Director of Administration

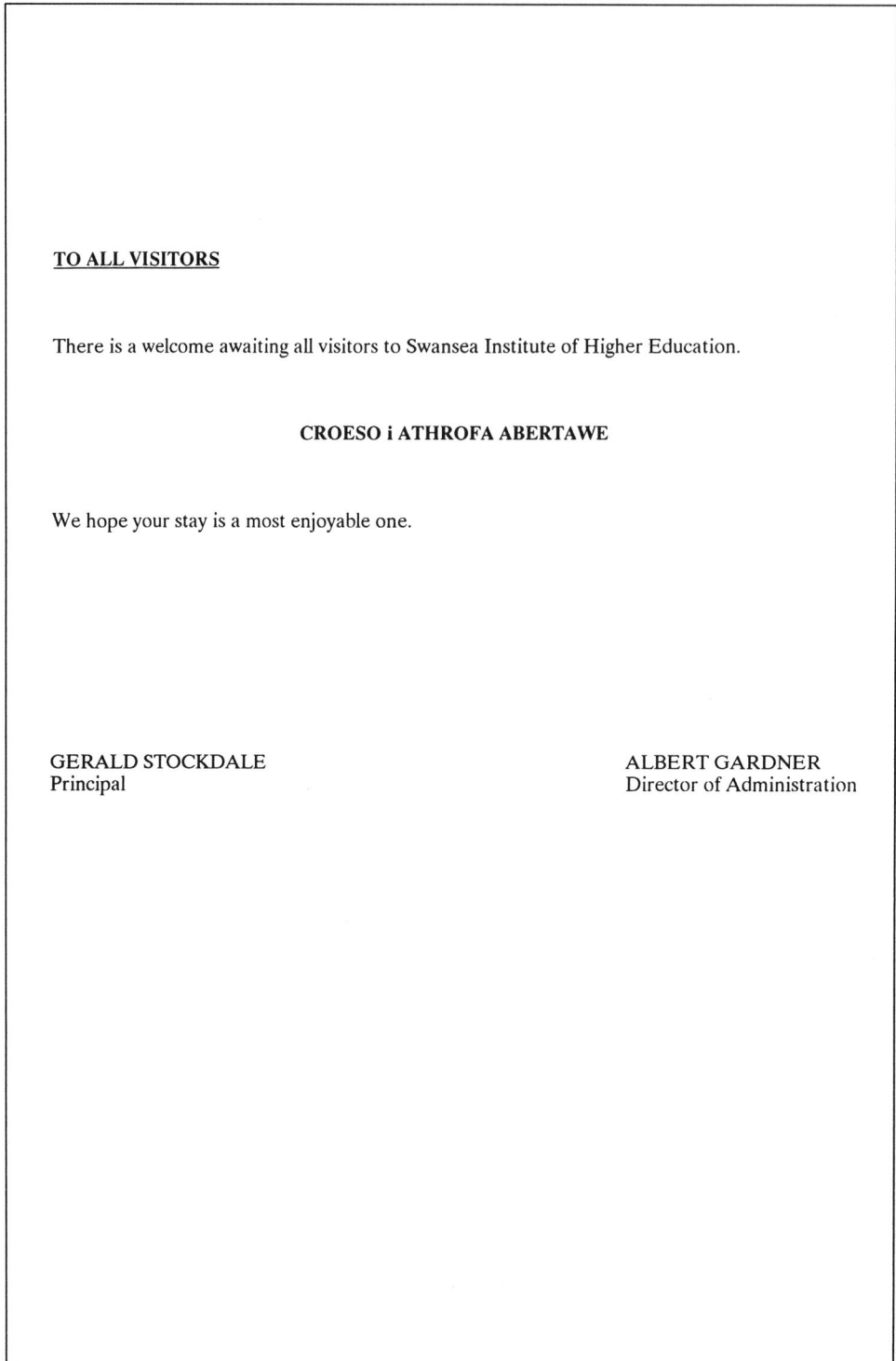

Figure 5.5   Venue information pack (continued)

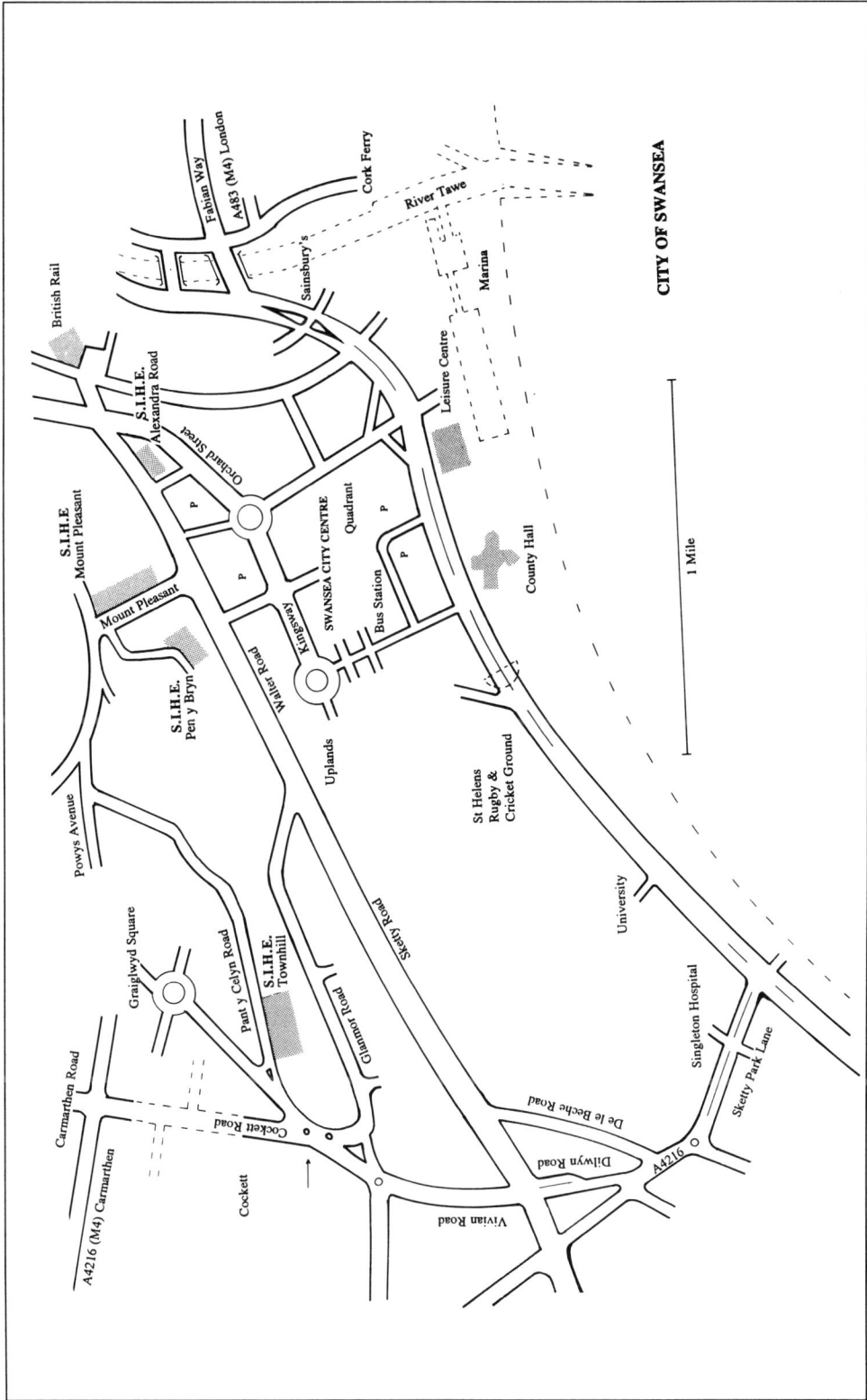

Figure 5.5 Venue information pack (concluded)

☐ Administrative assistance	☐ Notepads
☐ Blinds	☐ Parking facilities
☐ Boards (black, dry wipe, magnetic, white)	☐ Partitions
☐ Breakout rooms	☐ Pencils
	☐ Pens (highlighter, marker)
☐ Camcorders	☐ Photocopiers
☐ Cassette recorders	☐ Podia
☐ Chairs	☐ Pointers (laser, retractable)
☐ Cloakrooms	☐ Porters (day, night)
☐ Computers	☐ Posts
☐ Curtains (blackout, remote control)	☐ Projectors (film, overhead, slide)
	☐ Ropes
☐ Desks	☐ Safes
☐ Disabled facilities	☐ Screens
☐ Display boards	☐ Secretarial assistance
	☐ Shredders
☐ Easels	☐ Sockets (power, telephone)
☐ Extension leads	☐ Soundproofing
	☐ Stages
☐ Fax machines	
☐ Flip-charts	☐ Tables
☐ Foyer space	☐ Technicians
	☐ Telephones
☐ Gavels	☐ Televisions
	☐ Telex machines
☐ Heating (central, fan)	☐ Toilets
	☐ Translators
☐ Interpreters	☐ Tripods
	☐ Trolleys
☐ Kitchen space	☐ Typewriters
☐ Laminators	
☐ Lecterns (free-standing, table-top)	☐ Video players
	☐ Video recorders
☐ Lifts	
☐ Lighting (dimmer, fluorescent, remote control, spot, tungsten)	☐ Wall coverings
	☐ Word processors
☐ Medical services	
☐ Microphones (hand, lapel, stand)	And many more

Figure 5.6   Venue facilities and services: a checklist

available? Is there a technician on-site to operate them on your behalf? What other equipment are you looking for?

See Figure 5.6 above for a fuller checklist of facilities, services and equipment which may be available.

Is the venue available on your preferred dates?

If so, it could be that no one else wants it. Think about why this is – is it a poor venue, perhaps? If this is the case, what should you do? Would it be sensible or possible to rearrange your dates? Is there another, equally good venue which is available on your dates?

What are the costs involved?

What is included in the basic hire charge? More important, what is *not* included? Be clear about this now rather than later! Consider whether the figure is acceptable and within your budgetary constraints. How much do you have to pay for the extra facilities and services which are not part of the basic hire charge, such as the equipment, technician, and the time taken to set up and remove all the conference equipment?

Is there a conference executive (or a similarly titled person) available to assist you with your plans?

If there is, this implies you are likely to be dealing with a venue which takes conferences seriously. It may also indicate that you are going to receive individual attention – hard, practical advice geared to your particular situation. If not, it may be that conferences do not have a high priority with this venue and you will have to work with one person (or perhaps more than one) who has other tasks and duties to perform – probably someone who has no real knowledge of or interest in conferences!

Does the venue have a track record of staging conferences?

If so, can you contact the organizers of these events to ask whether they were happy with the venue and if they can recommend it to you? If not, you may be the first one to want to hold a conference there. Should you proceed on this basis in view of all of the (inevitable) first-time errors and mishaps that will occur?

Is suitable overnight accommodation available on-site or nearby?

Don't overlook this factor as many organizers tend to do. Refer to Figure 5.7 on page 66 for a fuller list of facilities, services and equipment that may be required. First, check that the accommodation is sited within a convenient walking or driving distance from the venue.

☐ Administrative assistance	☐ Medical services
☐ Baby items (cots, high chairs)	☐ Notepads
☐ Baby listening	☐ Parking facilities
☐ Banking facilities	☐ Pencils
☐ Bars (public, mini)	☐ Pens (ballpoints, fountain)
☐ Bathrobes	☐ Photocopiers
☐ Bookshops	☐ Porters (day, night)
☐ Call systems (early morning,	
☐ telephone)	☐ Radios
☐ Cassette recorders	☐ Refrigeration
☐ CD players	☐ Room service
☐ Chairs	
☐ Children's play areas	☐ Safes
☐ Computers	☐ Secretarial assistance
☐ Crèches	☐ Shredders
	☐ Smoking, non-smoking areas
☐ Desks	☐ Sockets (power, telephone)
☐ Disabled people's facilities	☐ Soundproofing
	☐ Study areas
☐ En-suite facilities	
	☐ Tables
☐ Fax machines	☐ Tea-, coffee-making facilities
	☐ Telex machines
☐ Games rooms	☐ Telephones (direct dial)
☐ General stores	☐ Televisions (satellite, terrestrial)
	☐ Toiletries
☐ Hairdressers	☐ Trolleys
☐ Hairdryers	☐ Trouser presses
☐ Health and beauty salons	☐ Typewriters
☐ Heating (central, fan)	
☐ Hi-fi systems	☐ Video players
	☐ Video recorders
☐ Kitchen space	☐ Videos
	☐ Views
☐ Laundry services	
☐ Leisure facilities	☐ Word processors
☐ Lifts	
☐ Lighting (dimmer, fluorescent,	And many more
remote control, spot, tungsten)	
☐ Living-room areas	

Figure 5.7 Overnight accommodation facilities and services: a checklist

Then, make sure that there are enough rooms of the right type free on your dates – singles and twins, doubles or family rooms. Are there ground-floor rooms for disabled participants? Are they of a standard which will satisfy or (better still) impress speakers, delegates and partners?

Are the required mix of facilities and services provided, such as ensuite facilities, mini bar, and study area in the rooms and a bar, restaurant, swimming pool, sauna or solarium in the hotel itself?

Will the costs incurred include room, breakfast, lunch, evening meal? Which facilities and services are incorporated within these costs and which are extras? How much do the extras cost?

Visiting venues

Now visit your shortlisted venues and any hotels which might provide overnight accommodation so that you can check the answers to your questions and make your final choices. Focus on the following areas and queries in particular.

Is the conference executive helpful?

Is he or she experienced and in control? More specifically, does he or she know what can and cannot be done on site? Ask if you can put up signs in the car park, decorate the foyer with banners or place a registration desk by the entrance. Find out if this is physically possible at that venue.

He or she may be able to advise you on your programme, make constructive criticisms, offer helpful suggestions and show you how it can be improved at this venue. Is he or she responsive to your wants and needs?

Do you have confidence in him or her? Does he or she make sense? Do you trust him or her? Do you believe what is being said? If the event is some time away, it is equally important to get to know, and have confidence in, other personnel at the venue. If the conference executive leaves before your event, it may be one of these staff who will take over.

Are the conference rooms right for you?

Are the entrances, heights, lengths, widths, obstructions, power points and exits all satisfactory? Measure them. Are lighting, heating and ventilation all suitable – in a blazing hot summer or in a freezing cold winter? Check them out. Noise levels are often overlooked. Inside the building, can your conference run without interruptions and distractions from others at the venue? Is it quiet enough outside the building, or will traffic, roadworks or any other noisy interruptions be off-putting for speakers and delegates.

Are you happy with the facilities, services and equipment on offer?

Are the facilities of a good quality, up to date and in a satisfactory condition?

Are you equally satisfied with the services that are being provided for you? For example, is the secretarial service up to your required standard and can the translator do his or her job well? Do you have faith in them?

Is the equipment solid and reliable, modern, in good condition and just what you want?

Are the hotel rooms right for participants?

Are they clean, tidy, comfortable and luxurious – will they satisfy speakers, delegates and partners or even impress them? Are the facilities and services all in order – the shower working properly, the mini-bar stocked and offering a good range of drinks? Is the bar pleasant and relaxing? Does the restaurant have a good choice of food? What else?

Is this the best deal for you?

If you can give positive answers to all the questions you have raised, then proceed. If not, consider looking elsewhere. If this venue represents value for money, then go ahead. If not, think again!

Making a provisional booking

You should now feel ready to make a provisional booking both at your selected venue and for overnight accommodation too, whether this is on the same site or elsewhere. There are a number of steps you should follow at this stage.

Have you discussed all aspects of your event with the conference executive?

Have you covered your objectives, who is coming, what they want and expect, how many will be there, the type of conference, the message, when you want to hold the event and how it will be conducted? Is there anything else?

Discuss also the money you are willing to spend at the venue, the basic hire charge, add-ons, facilities, services, equipment, technicians, and other relevant matters.

Talk to him or her, too, about your overall programme, the theme, your proposed business activities, the planned social activities and how they will fit together.

Have you also talked about *and* checked all aspects of the venue? Overnight accommodation as well?

Accessibility   On foot, by car and by public transport?

Size   The capacity of the rooms, their dimensions, access to them, lighting, heating and ventilation and noise levels?

Everything else on offer   Facilities, services and equipment and the availability of the venue on your preferred dates and on other dates?

Costs   Basic hire, add-ons and any other issues relevant to you?

Track record   Positive or negative response from previous users?

Overnight accommodation   Its accessibility, the number and type of rooms, standards, mix of facilities and services and costs?

Have you studied the venue's conditions of hire and code of practice, as relevant?

Look at Figures 5.8 and 5.9 on pages 70–78 and 79–80, which are typical examples of these documents.

Conditions of hire   Have you read each and every condition and sought a second opinion where necessary? Are you happy with these terms and conditions – are they fair and reasonable and can you abide by them? What about those which are not fair and reasonable or which you cannot abide by? If they are not negotiable, should you look elsewhere?

Code of practice   Have you considered all the clauses contained in this document and spoken to others about them (previous users of the

The Council of the Borough of Harrogate

The Harrogate Centre.

Conditions of Hire

Figure 5.8   Conditions of hire

Conditions of Hire

Interpretation

1. Throughout these Conditions where reference is made to any statute, regulations, byelaw or otherwise by name or implication these Conditions shall be read, construed and take effect as if they referred by name to the respective statute, regulations, byelaw or otherwise in force at the date of the Hiring Agreement including any amendments then current.

Throughout these Conditions the following expressions shall have the meanings assigned to them:

"Basic staffing complement" means one stage manager, one sound engineer, one lighting engineer, one front of house manager and a maximum of four doormen; for concerts a sufficient number of usherettes will be included; and basic staffing will be construed accordingly.

"Centre" means the Harrogate Centre or any part and includes all rooms, halls, corridors, lifts, stairways, cloakrooms, lavatories, and conveniences used or to be used by a Hirer or person authorised by him on the occasion of any hiring but does not include the restaurant, kitchen or bars.

"The Council" means the Council of the Borough of Harrogate including any Committee, Sub-Committee or Officer appointed by the Council for the purpose of management of the Harrogate Centre.

"Director" means the Council's Director of Resort Services for the time being or any person authorised by the Director or the Council to act on his behalf.

"Function" includes any kind of event or purpose for which the Centre is to be used by the Hirer.

"Hirer" means the person who has made application (whether personally or through an agent) to use the Centre and includes his agent and any other person employed by him (whether as servant or independent contractor) or acting under his direction.

"Hiring Agreement" means the agreement entered into between the Council and the Hirer setting out the period of hire and other details and incorporating these Conditions of Hire by reference.

"Hiring charge" means the sum ascertainable from the Hiring Agreement as the cost of hire of the Centre and does not include any additional costs to be charged as a result of requests made to the Director under these Conditions or otherwise unless the contrary appears from the Hiring Agreement.

"Period of hire" means the time during which the Hirer has contractual license to use the Centre under the Hiring Agreement including the period during which he requires access to make all preparations necessary for the function, the duration of the function and the time agreed thereafter for removing all materials, equipment etc. used for the purposes of the function.

Details of function

2. A complete programme of the function shall be delivered to the Director as soon as possible and in any case not less than seven days before the commencement of the period of hire.

In the event of the Hirer wishing to promote an exhibition he must submit a scale plan of the proposed layout of the exhibition to the Director for approval before agreements are made with the exhibitors. The plan will be submitted by the Director to the County Fire Officer for approval. No alterations may be made to the plan after it has been approved by the Director except with his written permission and the exhibition shall be laid out and maintained entirely in accordance with the approved plan.

Figure 5.8 Conditions of hire (continued)

Conditions of Hire

The Hirer shall notify the Director in writing not less than twelve weeks before the date of the function if it is intended to show films or video tapes at the function. Details must be given as to the type of film stock and projection equipment and/or video tape and recorder which it is proposed to use and whether members of the audience will be charged for admission either by programme or ticket. No entertainment for which a licence under the Cinematograph Acts is required may be given in the Centre unless the Hirer has first obtained the requisite licence. The Hirer shall be responsible for ensuring compliance with the terms of such licence.

In the event of the Centre being used by the Hirer for a conference the numbers of delegates who attended shall be supplied by the Hirer to the Director not more than seven days after the final day of that conference.

Advertising

3. If the Director so requires, the Hirer shall submit to him a draft of any poster, notice, bill, programme, announcement, advertisement or invitation relating to a function for which the Centre has been hired and shall comply with all requirements which the Director may reasonably impose.

No posters, notices or bills may be displayed inside or outside the Centre except by permission of the Director. The display of a reasonable number of approved posters or notices will be permitted on condition that the affixing and removal of same shall in no way affect, mark or damage the materials, fabric or decoration of the Centre internally or externally.

Tickets

4. Advance ticket sales shall be undertaken by the Director at the Centre Box Office and/or other offices under the control of the Council for all functions to which the general public is to be admitted unless the Hirer has obtained written permission to the contrary from the Director.

The Box Office in the Centre shall be manned by Council staff, unless written consent to the contrary has been obtained from the Director, and the Hirer shall pay for their services at the rates in force at the date of the Hiring Agreement.

When tickets are to be sold under this Condition printing will be undertaken by the Director at the expense of the Hirer.

In the case of functions so approved for the purposes of this Condition by the Director, the Hirer will be permitted to arrange the printing and sale of his own tickets. In such cases the tickets must conform to a prescribed pattern, details of which can be obtained from the Director.

The number of complimentary tickets to be issued by the Hirer for any function shall be subject to agreement by the Director.

Reservations for the Council

5. The Hirer shall reserve for the Council seats A1-A4 in Block E, seats A10-A13 in Block F and seats H1-H14 in Block G, all seat numbers inclusive, in respect of any function to which the general public is to be admitted and the Hirer shall deliver to the Director as soon as they are received from the printers the tickets for the seats which have been so reserved.

Care of the Centre

6. The Hirer may not place on or affix to the outside or inside of the Centre or bring into the Centre any furniture, fittings or temporary structures, except with the written permission of the Director.

Where the Centre is used for an exhibition all stands shall be of modular construction and approved by the Director in advance. No painting of stands or displays shall be permitted within the Centre. Where any machinery is to be displayed adequate protection must be afforded to walls and floor coverings in order to prevent wear and tear and damage from leakage or otherwise.

Figure 5.8   Conditions of hire (continued)

Conditions of Hire

In no circumstances shall any nails, screws, staples or pins of any kind be fixed into any part of the Centre, or its furniture, fittings or fixtures. Nothing may be displayed on or affixed to the walls of the Centre without the consent of the Director.

On termination of the hiring for any reason whatsoever whether before or after the function for which the Centre has been hired all machinery, equipment, furniture, fittings, stalls, stands, displays or other materials or exhibits brought into the Centre for the purposes of the function or displayed on or affixed to any part of the Centre shall be removed by the Hirer in such a way that no part of the Centre its fixtures, fittings or decoration whether internal or external is affected, marked or damaged in any way and any part of the Centre its fixtures, fittings or decoration which is so affected, marked or damaged shall be restored by the Council to the condition in which it was at the time of commencement of the period of hire and the cost to the Council of such restoration will be recharged to the Hirer.

Electrical Wiring and Fittings

7. The Hirer shall not interfere, nor permit any interference with any of the electrical wiring, installations or fittings of the Centre.

No electrical or other wiring (e.g. telephone - shortwave - amplification etc.) or electrical or other equipment or apparatus of any kind is to be placed in the Centre without the prior written consent of the Director.

Directional adjustment of the foyer light fittings will be carried out by the Council at the request of the Hirer and the cost of such adjustment and readjustment to the original setting will be charged to the Hirer at the rates in force at the date of the Hiring Agreement.

Where not already provided in the Centre a three-phase supply will be laid on by the Council at the request of the Hirer and the cost will be charged to the Hirer at the rates in force at the date of the Hiring Agreement.

Fire Precautions

8. All scenery, effects, properties, cloths, materials, stands and decorative displays must be rendered and maintained non-inflammable and must be declared to and approved by the County Fire Officer or his representative not less than seven days before the start of the function for which the Centre has been hired.

Any effects, properties, cloths, materials, stands and decorative displays which cannot be rendered non-inflammable under the preceding paragraph shall be declared to the Chief Fire Officer not less than one month before the period of hire commences and the Hirer shall comply with any requirement or recommendation of the Chief Fire Officer in respect of such effects, properties, cloths, materials, stands and decorative displays affecting safety, fire prevention or related matters.

Seating

9. The Centre is let with full seating and the Hirer will be responsible for all costs incurred in the removal, storage and replacement of any seating not required for the Hirer's function at the rates in force at the date of the Hiring Agreement.

The Council will use its best endeavours to arrange seating in accordance with the Hirer's requirements provided reasonable notice of such requirements has been given to the Director.

The Hirer must not issue tickets for admission to the function in excess of the seating capacity of the Centre for that function. In no circumstances may the Hirer admit to the function a greater number of persons than the number of seats provided in the Centre for that function.

Where the Director considers it to be necessary to fix a limit to the number of persons to be admitted to any function, the Hirer must not admit a greater number of persons than that specified by the Director.

Figure 5.8 Conditions of hire (continued)

Conditions of Hire

Compliance with Statutes etc.

10. The Hirer shall comply fully with all statutes, rules, regulations, orders, byelaws, or other requirements whether for ensuring public order, safety or decency or for any other purpose whatsoever affecting the use of the Centre for the purpose for which it has been hired, and with all requirements of the Health and Safety Executive, of the Police and Fire Authorities and of the Council including these Conditions and the duty to obtain all licences, consents and approvals necessary for the function.

All obligations, stipulations and Conditions to be observed on the part of the Hirer shall apply equally to the Hirer's servants, agents, contractors, sub-licensees and visitors (insofar as the same are relevant) and the Hirer shall be responsible for ensuring their compliance.

Right of Entry

11. The Council reserves for the Director the right of entry to the Centre during the period of hire to view the premises, the arrangements made for the proper supervision of the function and for any other reason or purpose which he may think proper in the interests of the Council, the Centre or Council staff.

Good Order

12. No impropriety of language, dress, dance, gesture or personality shall be permitted at any function and the Hirer shall to the best of his ability maintain and keep good order and decent behaviour in the Centre throughout the period of hire.

The Council reserves the right for the Director to refuse admission to, or to remove from the Centre any person who, in his opinion, is disorderly or objectionable.

The Hirer must inform every entertainer or group of entertainers that his or their performance must not be conducted in such a way that it may incite the audience to behave in a manner which may result in damage to the property of the Council or in a breach of public order, safety regulations or these Conditions and that members of the audience are not permitted to dance in the gangways or between the seats, but must remain seated throughout the performance.

Staffing

13. (a) Basic staffing will be provided at the Centre by the Council for the duration of the period of hire or as considered necessary by the Director.

Any staff required by the Hirer in addition to the basic staffing complement if requested in writing not less than seven days before the date of the function will be provided at the cost of the Hirer at the rates in force at the date of the Hiring Agreement.

(b) The Hirer must provide, at his own expense, Stewards of such a number as the Director may consider necessary for the proper conduct of the function.

All Stewards must be and remain on duty at the Centre for the period specified by the Director and must be instructed that they are to comply with any requirement of the Director.

(c) For all functions in the Centre to which the general public is to be admitted the Director will provide a sufficient number of trained Security Personnel to meet the demands of the particular function as anticipated by the Director in consultation with the Hirer but in default of agreement as fixed by the Director. Security Personnel will be provided at the cost of the Hirer at the rates in force at the date of the Hiring Agreement.

(d) At the discretion of the Director cloakroom facilities with attendants will be provided.

(e) If the Hirer shall so request the Director he shall use his best endeavours to provide any additional staff notwithstanding that it may be outside normal working hours and the Council shall be entitled to charge for such staff at the rates in force at the date of the Hiring Agreement.

Police and Firemen

14. The Hirer will be charged for any attendance of the Police or Fire Service which the Director shall judge to be necessary.

Figure 5.8   Conditions of hire (continued)

Conditions of Hire

Collections

15. The collection of money whether for charitable or any other purpose from those attending the function is not permitted without the prior written consent of the Director.

Sales of chattels and programmes

16. No chattel or real property may be raffled, sold or offered for sale whether by auction or otherwise in the Centre, with the following exceptions:

    (a) the sale of programmes catalogues or other literature or articles ancillary to the function.
    (b) where the sale of chattels or real property is the express or implied object of the function.
    (c) sales expressly authorised in writing by the Director prior to the function.

    Rates of commission on all sales must be approved by the Director prior to the function.

Copyright

17. No copyright work shall be performed other than
    (a) such as is authorised by the current licence of the Performing Rights Society Limited a copy of which can be inspected at the Centre on request and shall be deemed to have been read by the Hirer,

    (b) any work in respect of which the licence of the owner of the copyright for the performance is produced to the Director before the commencement of the function, and the Hirer shall indemnify the Council against all costs, claims and liability in respect of the performance of any copyright work not so authorised.

    For the purpose of this clause "copyright" includes the copyright subsisting in a film video tape recording or broadcast as such but not the copyright subsisting in a recording (not being a film video tape recording or broadcast) as such. References to the performance of a copyright work shall be deemed to include the playing or reproduction of the work by means of a recording or any other means whatsoever.

    A Hirer shall, within seven days of the date of a function, render the Director a return in duplicate on the form provided of all works performed in the Centre during the period of hire.

Amplification and relay equipment

18. A Hirer who wishes to make use of any equipment installed in the Centre for the purpose of sound amplification or relaying shall make arrangements for the same with the Director.

Recording/reproduction broadcast etc. of entertainment.

19. The Hirer must not record, transmit or broadcast, or permit to be recorded, transmitted or broadcast by telegraph, telephone, radio, television, video tape or any other means, any performance, entertainment, or the subject matter of any function, except with the previous written consent of the Director and on such terms as may be approved by him.

    The Hirer must not reproduce whether aurally or visually, or permit the aural or visual reproduction of any performance or entertainment or the subject matter of any function except with the prior written permission of the Director and on such terms as may be approved by him.

    No photograph, film or video tape recording may be taken or made in the Centre without the prior written permission of the Director and on such terms as may be approved by him.

Refreshments

20. The Council reserves for its own exclusive benefit all bars and refreshment rooms with the right to sell and provide all refreshments whether solid or liquid including wines beers, spirits and other alcoholic liquors to be consumed in the Centre and to provide such catering facilities as it may in its absolute discretion think fit

Cleaning

21. (a) The Hirer will leave the Centre and all its fittings, fixtures, furniture, apparatus and equipment in a reasonably clean condition. If the Director is not satisfied with the condition of the Centre or the said fittings, fixtures, furniture, apparatus and equipment at the expiration of the period of hire, the Hirer will be required to reimburse the Council for the cost of cleaning to a standard satisfactory to the Director.

Figure 5.8 Conditions of hire (continued)

Conditions of Hire

(b) The Hirer will be required to ensure that all structures, goods and chattels erected in or brought into the Centre during the period of hire and all residual rubbish and debris are removed from the Centre by the expiration of the period of hire so that the Centre when vacated is left in a clean and orderly state. In the event of the Hirer failing to comply with his obligations under this Condition the Council or the Director shall be entitled to put the Centre into a clean and orderly state and, where necessary, to place any such structures, goods and chattels in store and the cost to the Council of securing compliance with this Condition will be charged to the Hirer as an additional charge including any transportation and storage costs.

Exclusion of Liability

22. The Council will not be responsible for any article of any kind which is brought into or left in the Centre.

Where the Hirer is in breach of his obligations under Condition 21 and the Director is thereby required to exercise his powers under 21(b) the Hirer shall not hold the Council or the Director responsible in any way for any loss which may occur to the Hirer due to any failure on the part of the Director to distinguish between items requiring storage and items requiring destruction.

Any structures, goods or chattels which are placed in store under Condition 21 will be held by the Council to the order of the Hirer and at his sole risk.

Indemnity

23. The Hirer will be liable for any damage done to or loss of any property of the Council or for which the Council is responsible under the law, arising out of the hire of the Centre whether caused by the Hirer or by any other persons using the Centre as a result of the Hiring Agreement.

Liability under this Condition shall exclude loss or damage caused to the building (but not its fixtures, fittings or equipment) to the extent that it is insured by the Council.

In the event of any damage or loss being sustained, suffered or incurred by the Hirer or any other person due to any breakdown of machinery, failure of supply of electricity, leakage of water, fire, government restriction or act of God or to the temporary closing of the Centre or the interruption of the period of hire by circumstances beyond the control of the Council or to any other cause whatsoever the Hirer shall accept full responsibility and shall indemnify the Council against all costs, claims, demands and expenses arising. Provided that this Condition shall not apply to personal injury, damage or loss or to any claim caused by the negligence of any servant of the Council arising out of the performance of his duties as such servant.

Insurance

24. Without prejudice to the generality of Condition 10 to comply with all statutes, rules, regulations, orders, byelaws or other requirements whether for public safety or otherwise and without prejudice to the generality of the other Conditions relating to the liability of the Hirer to the Council for the conduct of the function and the care of the Centre its fixtures fittings and equipment, the Hirer shall procure public liability insurance cover for the period of hire in the sum of four million pounds and shall produce evidence to the Director not less than seven days before the commencement of the period of hire.

Anticipatory Breach

25. The Council reserves the right to cancel any function if in the opinion of the Director:
(a) the Hirer intends to use the Centre for any purpose other than the purpose specified in the Hiring Agreement.

(b) the Hirer intends to use the Centre for a public entertainment in respect of which a licence under the Cinematograph Acts is required, and the Hirer has not obtained the requisite licence.

(c) the function may lead to a breach of the peace or acts of violence may occur or damage may be caused to the Centre or any of its fixtures, fittings or decoration.

(d) the nature of the function or of any item in the programme is such as to render it undesirable that it should be in a building under the control of the Council.

Figure 5.8   Conditions of hire (continued)

Conditions of Hire

In the event of the function being cancelled as provided above, or being cancelled by the Hirer in circumstances in which the Council is unable to re-let the Centre, the Council reserves the right:

(a) to retain any deposit or sum of money that may have been paid by the Hirer; and

(b) to claim any balance of the hiring charge payable under the Hiring Agreement; and

(c) to claim any other expenses incurred by the Council in connection with the function.

Cancellation by the Director

26. The Council reserves the right to cancel any function if in the opinion of the Director:

   (a) it is necessary to close the Centre for the purpose of executing urgent repairs.

   (b) it is in the public interest that the Centre shall be closed on any day for which the function has been arranged.

   (c) the Centre has been rendered unfit for use by reason of flood, tempest, storm, fire, electrical or mechanical breakdown or other cause beyond the Council's control.

   (d) the Centre is required for some public or civic purpose. (As far as possible periods of hire will be arranged so as not to conflict with civic requirements).

   (e) there is in existence an industrial dispute rendering the holding of the function inadvisable.

   In the event of any function being cancelled as provided above, the Hirer shall be repaid any deposit or sum of money that may have been paid for the period of the cancellation but shall have no claim against the Council for any damage or loss which he may sustain or have sustained nor in respect of any liability which he may incur or have incurred in consequence of such cancellation.

Cancellation by the Hirer

27. If the Hirer shall cancel the function the Council shall be entitled to the whole of the hiring charge together with a sum equal to any costs borne by the Council in connection with the function up to the date of the Hirer's cancellation Provided Always that if notice of the cancellation is received by the Council prior to the date on which the period of hire would otherwise have commenced then if the Council shall find another Hirer for the whole or part of the Centre the Hirer shall be liable to pay only for that part of the Centre and only for that period of hire which have not been taken over by such other Hirer.

Breach of Conditions of Hire

28. In the event of the Hirer failing to observe and perform or failing to cause to be observed and performed any of these Conditions the Council may, without prejudice to any right of action which it may have against the Hirer, forthwith and without prior notice to the Hirer cancel the function and, if necessary, require him to vacate the Centre and in the event of any function being cancelled the Council shall be entitled to retain any deposit or other payments he may have made and the Hirer shall have no claim against the Council for any damage or loss he may sustain or have sustained nor in respect of any liability which he may incur or have incurred in consequence of such cancellation.

Bankruptcy etc.

29. In the event of a Hirer committing any act of bankruptcy or (being a Company) entering into liquidation either compulsorily or voluntarily the function shall be automatically cancelled and in the event of any function being so cancelled the Council shall be entitled to retain any deposit or sum of money that may have been paid and the Hirer his Trustee in Bankruptcy, Receiver or Liquidator shall have no claim against the Council in respect of such cancellation or any damage or loss which he may sustain or have sustained nor in respect of any liability which he may incur or have incurred in consequence of such cancellation.

Figure 5.8   Conditions of hire (continued)

Conditions of Hire

Tenure

30. Nothing in these Conditions shall be construed as conferring upon the Hirer any rights of occupation or use of the Centre other than a personal licence for the purpose described in the Hiring Agreement.

   The Hirer shall not assign the benefit of the Hiring Agreement to any other person or persons nor assign nor sub-licence any right or benefit under it.

Payment

31. A deposit of one third of the hiring charge is payable to the Council on remitting the signed copy of the Hiring Agreement to the Council.

   Where appropriate the Director reserves the right to demand in advance the total installation charge and a sum to cover the estimated cost of additional water, electricity gas or other services laid on for the function at the request of the Hirer.

   All sums to be paid by or charged to the Hirer under the Hiring Agreement or by reason of these Conditions shall be deemed to be a debt due and payable to the Council from the Hirer as from the date of invoice or other notification of the amount due.

   All sums due by the Hirer to the Council shall be paid without any deduction except as required by law or by any provision in the Hiring Agreement in pounds sterling in Harrogate converted at the official rate of exchange at the date of the payment.

Variation of Hiring Agreement

32. The Hiring Agreement can only be varied with the consent of the Director and an application to vary must be made in writing to the Director at least 30 days before the period of hire commences.

Notices

33. Any notice or communication to be given under these Conditions may be sent by post to the address appearing in the Hiring Agreement or such other address as either the Council or the Hirer may from time to time have communicated in writing to the other in accordance with this Condition and if so sent shall be deemed to be received on the day following the date of posting. In proving service it shall be sufficient to show that the notice was properly addressed, stamped and posted by first class ordinary post.

Arbitration

34. If any dispute or difference shall arise between the Council and the Hirer with reference to the interpretation of the Hiring Agreement or any act, matter or thing to be done under the Hiring Agreement or any claim or demand arising, the same shall be dealt with under the Arbitration Act 1979 (which term shall include any Act amending or re-enacting the same) by an Arbitrator appointed in the event of disagreement by the President for the time being of the Law Society.

Lex fori

35. The Hiring Agreement shall be governed by English Law and shall be deemed to have been made in England.

Marginal Notes

36. The marginal notes in these Conditions are for convenience only and shall not affect the construction or interpretation of the Conditions.

Figure 5.8　Conditions of hire (concluded)

COUNCIL OF THE BOROUGH OF HARROGATE
CODE OF PRACTICE FOR USE OF HARROGATE INTERNATIONAL
CONFERENCE CENTRE

The following serve as reinforcement to the Conditions of Hire issued with the Contract for your use of the Conference Centre. Not all items necessarily apply to your event but must be adhered to when appropriate.
(There is no particular order of priority to this list.)

1   No signs, notices or posters to be affixed to the internal fabric of the building – all such signs/notices to be free-standing. In exceptional circumstances, Blu-tac or similar substances may be used on glass surfaces with the prior permission of the Event Manager responsible for your event. NB: "Sticky-Pads" are <u>NOT</u> acceptable at all. Permission to erect/display exterior signs must also be sought from the Event Manager.

2   Painting of construction materials/exhibition stands is prohibited in all carpeted areas. Where this is necessary in the Auditorium during set construction, steps <u>MUST BE</u> taken to protect the flooring by use of suitable material, eg plastic sheeting. N.B. Painting is not allowed at all in the two foyer levels.

3   Sections of stage sets/lighting rigs <u>MUST NOT</u> be placed on the backs of Auditorium seating whilst awaiting use – they should, where possible, be placed on the floor. If, however, sheer size restricts this, suitable protection <u>MUST BE</u> placed on the seating in question and only under guidance by the Department of Resort Services Stage Manager.

4   Any scaffolding or other temporary structures/platforms <u>CAN ONLY</u> be constructed in seated areas using previously approved materials under the supervision of Department of Resort Services technical staff.

5   The utmost care <u>MUST BE</u> taken when transporting equipment and containers around the building, especially with regard to doors, doorways, stairways, corridor walls and carpeted areas. Particular care must be taken when it is necessary to transfer stand materials between the two foyer levels using either the ramp or the escalator, as ceiling levels vary quite significantly. Please note weight limit in the two passenger lifts (900 kg each) – any costs incurred due to overloading will be recharged.

6   The permanently let display cases on both foyer levels must not be obscured by stands or display materials; and the mobile catering/bar counters situated in these foyers may only be used with the permission of the Department of Resort Services Commercial Manager. Display materials, banners, etc. must not be attached to the window blinds in these two areas under any circumstances.

Figure 5.9   Code of practice

7   Cooking <u>IS NOT</u> allowed inside the building other than in the purpose-built kitchen attached to the Centre Restaurant and under the strict control of the Commercial Manager or the Buffet Area in Exhibition Hall D, if available. Any other arrangements must take place outside, in suitable vehicles. This applies particularly to crew catering connected with travelling entertainment events.

8   Food and drink <u>CANNOT</u> be consumed in the Auditorium at any time, including build-up and breakdown periods. Areas are provided back stage for crew refreshment breaks.

9   Fire exit signs <u>MUST NOT</u> be obscured. If the construction of a stage set is such that the exits on either side of the stage are covered, access <u>MUST BE</u> allowed around either end of the set and temporary directional signs fitted.

10   All aisles <u>MUST</u> remain free from encumbrance whilst delegates/audience occupy the Auditorium.

11   The unauthorised parking of vehicles on the paved area between the main entrance and the flagpoles is <u>STRICTLY PROHIBITED</u>.

Any damage caused to the fabric, furniture or fittings of the Conference Centre as a consequence of failure to observe these conditions will be restored by the Department of Resort Services and the cost recharged to the organiser of the event.

Figure 5.9   Code of practice (concluded)

venue, perhaps)? Do you feel comfortable with them and able to adhere to them? Are those that you are uncomfortable with applied on a rigorous basis and, if so, should you seek another venue?

Do you now feel able to complete a booking form?

See Figure 5.10 on pages 81–84 for an example of such a form. Are you aware of the information that needs to be provided at this stage?

You will need to provide on the booking form: the company's name, the conference organizer's name and title, address, telephone and fax numbers, date and time of arrival. State clearly the number of attendees, names and number of venue rooms required, days and times and numbers of delegates per room. List the equipment, facilities and services required, on which days and times. Specify your catering requirements. If overnight accommodation is needed, list the number and types of bedrooms, any further requirements, and the date and time of departure.

LOSEHILL HALL BOOKING FORM

Organisation/Name of Group _____

Name and Title of Organiser _____

Daytime Telephone Number of Organiser _____

Full Address _____

_____

_____ Postcode _____

Date of Arrival _____   Date of Departure _____

Time of Arrival _____   Time of Departure _____

Number of people attending _____

Number of bedrooms required: Twin Rooms _____ Single Rooms _____

Meeting Room required from (day and time) _____

Meeting Room required until (day and time) _____

The Meeting Room will be required for _____ people

If you require tables in your Meeting Room will these be used for:

    Display of publications etc (i.e. around the edge of the room)   ☐

    Seating purposes (arranged with chairs)   ☐

The Meeting Room should be set out in the following manner:

_____

If you would like a particular Meeting Room, if available, please specify

_____

Will you require any Seminar Rooms, if so how many and when?
(£40.00 per day)

_____

_____

Figure 5.10 Booking form

Please detail at what time you would like the following to be served each day:

Coffee and biscuits _____

Lunch _____

(or)

Packed Lunch _____

Afternoon tea and biscuits _____

If you would like the use of any equipment during your stay, please tick appropriate boxes.

16mm film projector ☐

Overhead projector ☐

35mm carousel projector ☐

Flip chart ☐

Whiteboard ☐

VHS Video recorder ☐

Do you have any further requirements? _____

_____

_____

How did you find out about Losehill Hall? _____

If you have stayed at the Hall before, during which year did you stay? _____

I have read and understand the Conditions of Booking given on Page 2

Signed_____   Date _____

Please return the completed form, together with your deposit or official order, to Mrs Pat Smith, Bookings Manager, Peak National Park Centre, Losehill Hall, Castleton, Derbyshire, S30 2WB. Telephone: Hope Valley (0433) 620373 Fax: Hope Valley (0433) 620346. Please make your cheque payable to the Peak Park Joint Planning Board.

Figure 5.10   Booking form (continued)

GROUP BOOKINGS - LIST OF PARTICIPANTS

NAME OF GROUP _____

DATES OF VISIT _____

PLEASE INDICATE WHETHER SINGLE OR TWIN ROOMS ARE REQUIRED
AND BRACKET TOGETHER THOSE PEOPLE WHO ARE TO SHARE

Male (M) Female (F)	FULL NAME (please print clearly)	CATEGORY OF ROOM REQUIRED	SPECIAL DIETS/ (e.g. vegetarian, vegan) MEDICAL CONDITIONS

Please return this section of the Booking Form (together with a course programme if you have one) as soon as possible.

Please return to Pat Smith, Bookings Manager, Peak National Park Centre, Losehill Hall, Castleton, Derbyshire, S30 2WB. Tel: Hope Valley (0433) 620373. Fax: (0433) 620346.

Figure 5.10 Booking form (continued)

Male (M) Female (F)	FULL NAME (please print clearly)	CATEGORY OF ROOM REQUIRED	SPECIAL DIETS/ (e.g. vegetarian, vegan) MEDICAL CONDITIONS

CONTINUATION SHEET

PLEASE INDICATE WHETHER SINGLE OR TWIN ROOMS ARE REQUIRED
AND BRACKET TOGETHER THOSE PEOPLE WHO ARE TO SHARE

Figure 5.10   Booking form (concluded)

In an accompanying letter give any basic information not requested in the venue's booking form: confirmation and explanation of your extra requirements, free rehearsal time, perhaps, ongoing availability of the conference executive, use of a technician, costs involved, payment dates, terms and conditions, request for a written response agreeing to your requirements – especially those which vary from the conditions of hire.

What should you do on receipt of your booking confirmation and perhaps a formal contract?

Refer to Figures 5.11 and 5.12 on pages 86–89 and 90 respectively, for examples of these items.

Are the details listed in the booking confirmation absolutely correct? Surprisingly, they are often not 100 per cent accurate. Amend incorrect text, initial alterations and draw attention to them, in a separate explanatory letter, if necessary. More important, make sure *all* the information is included, especially those extra requirements requested in your earlier letter. Take nothing for granted – ensure that everything is put in writing now! You will probably have to pay a deposit at this stage.

A formal contract may be necessary for some venues, but not all, so do check. If so, ensure that every single key detail is included, or attach an additional sheet for both parties to sign. If all the clauses are not clear and specific, add an extra, explanatory comment to be initialled by both sides.

What happens after these documents have been completed?

Confirm any outstanding details in writing, as soon as possible, giving the exact numbers of delegates, their wants and needs, any special requirements, details of facilities and services being provided by other suppliers and miscellaneous additional details.

Finalize the programme, including the business activities and social activities. Inform the venue of any alterations, especially those which affect it in particular. Send any documents and materials which may be of relevance, such as publicity material, to the conference executive and his or her staff.

Anything else? Check regularly to make certain that all is progressing well. Are there any queries, uncertainties or problems? Have another venue and overnight accommodation lined up just in case – definitely!

BOLTON INSTITUTE

Bolton Institute

Deane Road
Bolton, BL3 5AB
Tel. (0204) 28851
Fax. (0204) 399071

Ref:　　　　　　　　　　　　　　Date:

Dear

TITLE AND DATE OF CONFERENCE

Please find enclosed a confirmation of booking and estimation of cost for the period shown above.　A non-refundable deposit of £　　　　is now payable to secure your booking which will of course be deducted from your final account.

I also enclose a copy of our Terms & Conditions of Hiring Accommodation.　When you return the signed booking form and deposit, please also return a signed copy of the Terms & Conditions form.

If the Institute can be of any further assistance to you, please do not hesitate to contact me at the above address, or Telephone (0204) 28851, Extn 3126.

Yours sincerely

Joyce Proia
Conference Administrator
Residential Services

Enclosures

Principal R Oxtoby BSc MEd PhD CEng MInstE FIMgt FRSA, Bolton Institute of Higher Education, Deane Road, Bolton BL3 5AB

Figure 5.11　Confirmation of booking

CONFIRMATION OF BOOKING

BOLTON INSTITUTE OF HIGHER EDUCATION
CONFERENCE AND FACILITIES DEPARTMENT
DEANE
PHONE NO: 28851   EXT. 3124/26

ESTIMATE OF COST

Your booking for the period

.... to .... Site

for our ....

is confirmed.

A valid contract will exist when we have

received the 10% non-returnable booking fee

of £ ....

	Number of Persons	Number of Days	Number of Person/Days	Rate per Day	TOTAL £ p
Rooms					
Breakfast					
Lunch					
Dinner					
Coffee					
Tea					
Late Night Drinks					
Extras					
TOTALS					

VAT @   %

TOTAL

Booking Fee 10%

Figure 5.11 Confirmation of booking (continued)

TERMS OF CONDITIONS OF HIRING ACCOMMODATION
BOLTON INSTITUTE

DEFINITIONS

Bolton Institute of Higher Education hec is hereinafter referred to as **The Institute**, the Company or person hiring facilities and services is hereinafter referred to as **The Hirer**. The land and buildings to be occupied and/or used by the **The Hirer** are hereinafter called the **The Premises**. In the conditions of hire, the **The Hirer** shall mean the person signing the Booking form and where the person signing the form on behalf of an organisation, the organisation is also considered as the **The Hirer** and shall be jointly and severally liable.

CHARGES

The charges for the facilities and services at **The Premises** shall be in accordance with the Tariffs agreed with **The Institute** for the actual period of hire. All sums due shall be payable to **The Institute** in accordance with the payment details set out below. All cheques should be made payable to "Bolton Institute".

PAYMENT DETAILS

DAY CONFERENCES

Deposit of 20% upon placement of booking.
Full balance to be paid 10 days before event commences.

RESIDENTIAL EVENTS

A deposit of 20% payable upon placement of booking.
Full payment due 30days before commencement of event.

CANCELLATION

All cancellations must be in writing.
Cancellation charges shall apply if the booking is cancelled by
The Hirer, and charges will be as follows:-

Within four weeks of event commencement - 50% charge

Within 3 days of event commencement - 100% charge.

SUB LETTING

The Hirer shall not sub-let **The Premises** without prior agreement of **The Institute**.

RIGHT OF ENTRY

The Institute reserves the right of entry to the premises by its staff or agents or other authorised officers of **The Institute**

THE HIRER'S RESPONSIBILITIES

The Hirer shall be responsible for ensuring that persons brought to any part of the premises comply with Licensing and other statutory requirements to which **The Institute** and its servants or agents are subject. (A copy of **The Institute's** "Code of Practice" is available on request).

The Hirer shall be fully responsible for all persons and property brought on to the premises during the period of hire and shall indemnify **The Institute** against any loss or damage to property including property of The Institute. The Hirer agrees to undertake to pay the cost of making good damage that may occur, whether to buildings, fixture and fittings, furniture, piano apparatus, sports ground or otherwise and howsoever caused, by reason of such hiring.

The Institute reserves the right to terminate reservations at any time if **The Premises** are used for illegal purposes and in su an event will not be liable to refund any monies paid.

Figure 5.11   Confirmation of booking (continued)

The **Hirer** will be held responsible for the return of all Institute Keys. **The Institute** has a standard charge of thirty pounds (£30) payable by **The Hirer** for each lost key.

SMOKING POLICY

The Institute operates a non-smoking policy. There are however, designated areas, for those wishing to smoke. Smoking is allowed in designated accommodation. Fire Precaution notices are distributed in all buildings on the Campus, we ask that you instruct your delegates to read these instructional notices. We undertake Fire Drills periodically. Under no circumstances should Fire Alarms be ignored.

COMPLAINTS

Any complaint arising out of the hiring should be made in writing to **The Institute** within 3 days of the occasion of such complaint.

CUSTOMER CARE

You will be given a customer care form at the end of your event. Please help us by completing this.

I/We the undersigned agree to abide by and observe all the above conditions imposed by **The Institute** set out in the preceeding Terms and Conditions for the hire of Institute Premises and Services.

Signed ....

Date ....

On behalf of Organisation/Body ....

PLEASE COMPLETE AND RETURN THE TERMS AND CONDITIONS FORM WITH BOOKING FORM TO:

THE CONFERENCE ADMINISTRATOR
BOLTON INSTITUTE OF HIGHER EDUCATION hec
DEANE ROAD
BOLTON
BL3 5AB

7.3.94

Figure 5.11 Confirmation of booking (concluded)

Recommended reading

Kozicki, S. (1994), *The Creative Negotiator*, Gower, Aldershot.
Maddox, R.B. (1988), *Successful Negotiation*, Kogan Page, London.

H / 1   (HIR101)

AN AGREEMENT made the   day of   , 199
between the Council of the Borough of Harrogate (hereinafter called "the Council") of Council Offices,
Crescent Gardens, Harrogate under the hand of Paul Lewis its Director of Harrogate International Centre
and duly authorised agent of the first part AND -

(hereinafter called the Hirer) of

under the hand of

its/his/their duly authorised agent of the second part *WHEREBY IN CONSIDERATION* of an undertaking by the Hirer to comply with
the Conditions of Hire (a copy of which he confirms having received from the Council prior to the signing of this Agreement) and with the provisions of

this Agreement the Council *HEREBY GRANTS* to the Hirer a licence to use the following:

      PERIOD OF HIRE .. from 08:00 am on   199
                          to   11:59 pm on   199

      For :

Details of Hiring Charge:

      AT A TOTAL COST OF   £   PLUS VAT
      Payment of deposit of   PLUS VAT *to be made by*

      Additional Staffing costs :   As required
      Additional equipment or services : As required

IN WITNESS WHEREOF this Agreement has been executed by or on behalf of the Council and the Hirer the day and year first written:-

Signed by *PAUL LEWIS*   *SIGNED BY:*

Director of Harrogate International Centre   as agent duly authorised for and
and duly authorised agent of Harrogate   on behalf of the Hirer
Borough Council in the presence of:-   in the presence of:-

WITNESS: Name   *WITNESS: Name*
          Address   *Address*

Figure 5.12   Booking contract

6

Bringing in Speakers

You will have considered already who you want to speak at your conference when you set your initial framework of objectives to work within and towards. You now need to think about your prospective speakers in greater detail to make sure that you identify, find and sign up the right ones for your needs.

Identifying the right speakers

Clearly, your first task must be to identify the people you wish to talk at the event, lead a discussion, demonstrate goods and so on. The following questions should help you to recognize suitable people who can then be approached in due course.

Generally, who should you select to speak at a conference? What qualities are you looking for in speakers?

They should be people who are fully familiar with their subject matter and really know what they are talking about. You might also want them to be regarded as experts on that subject, and to have the respect of their audience. Ideally, they should be experienced and capable of doing what you want them to do – to make an interesting speech, control a lively discussion, handle tricky questions or demonstrate a product in a clear and concise manner. You might also need them to attract delegates to the event. Should they be a personality, then? In the trade? Locally or nationally famous?

Make a note of the particular qualities and attributes that will suit your purposes.

What should be the other main influences on your choice?

Your choice will be affected by the type of conference you are organizing. If it is an incentive event, consider whether the managing director should speak, to add prestige to the occasion. If it is a press conference, should public relations experts be drafted in?

What topics need to be covered: sales figures, facts about a revised product range? Is the message to be put over an informative or a persuasive one which might be most suited to the sales director, the marketing director or someone else, perhaps?

How much does your budget allow you to spend on speakers, fees, travel and accommodation expenses and miscellaneous extras? Be wary of exceeding your budget. If you do, can you make cutbacks elsewhere and what might be the consequences of any savings?

If you are aware of any other influences which are relevant to your particular situation, be conscious of them at all times.

How many speakers do you want to participate in your event? How do you decide?

Do you want just the managing director, or the sales director instead? If more than that, how many?

The number of speakers depends partly on your approach. Will your conference comprise a series of speeches made to all the delegates sitting together and, if so, can one person handle this? If you intend to set up discussions among smaller groups, then three or four people, or perhaps more, may be needed to manage them.

Consider how many delegates one speaker can address successfully. Find out the optimum size for a discussion group. How many speakers are needed to demonstrate goods, allowing time for delegates to examine them? How large should the groups be for demonstrations?

Take into account the length of the conference. If it is scheduled for just one afternoon can one person manage this on his or her own? If it is for a day, should the workload be shared out between two or more speakers, thus offering freshness and variety to their audience as well? You may need several speakers for a two- or three-day conference.

In practice, can you choose your speakers?

If so, you should look at all the questions above, answer them and build up a clear idea of the type and number of speakers you want. Do you have particular people in mind, ready to be contacted?

If not, has the managing director informed you that he or she intends to make all the speeches? Has the sales director 'suggested' that he or she will handle any discussions? Does this have a (painfully) familiar ring to it? You may just have to accept it! Can you bring in other, first-rate speakers as well, to enliven the proceedings and add interest and variety?

Finding speakers

With a better idea of the type and number of speakers required for the event you can set about finding the right people. Sometimes this will be relatively easy – you may know someone who seems ideal, or perhaps they have already approached you to announce their intention to play an active role in the conference whether you like it or not. On other occasions, suitable speakers may be harder to find, although there are various ways of approaching the task to increase your chances of success.

Have you considered everyone within your firm?

You   Could you become involved in some capacity, perhaps by making an opening speech, being on standby in case someone withdraws or is taken ill, or drawing the event to an end with a closing speech?

Your immediate colleagues   Would any of them be suitable as a speaker or to handle question-and-answer sessions? If not, they may know someone who could do a good job for you.

Someone further up or lower down in the organization   Don't be afraid to ask heads of other departments or directors. Don't overlook, either, staff lower down in the organization – juniors, part-timers or even temporary staff. They may be able to demonstrate products for you. If not, they may be a source of ideas and contacts. Don't be reluctant to speak to them!

How about outside the firm?

Business associates   Could they play a part in the proceedings? Perhaps they might enhance a promotional or press conference by talking about how happy they are with your products or services, or help out at a training event by showing how to use updated equipment, master a new task and so on. Can they also introduce you to additional, would-be speakers?

Other contacts   Have you thought whether friends and relatives could put you in touch with speakers, perhaps even local celebrities?

What about your sponsors? Can they help out at all?

Your professional association   Could they provide a speaker for a trade event or a list of people you can approach, such as well-known names in the trade or personalities?

The local Training and Enterprise Council   Might one of their team come to your training event to give a speech, perhaps? If not, they may be able to point you in the right direction.

The Department of Trade and Industry   Is someone available from a regional office to make a speech, possibly to overseas delegates? Or might they suggest other people who might participate instead?

Other businesses   Is another business staging a complementary exhibition alongside your conference? Would it be willing to put together a presentation of some kind on your behalf or share their contacts list with you?

Are there any other individuals or organizations that can help you?

The nearest tourist board could provide a speaker to outline the attractions in the area, perhaps to partners or to other speakers, delegates and partners during a lull in business activities. Find out if the tourist board can give you the names of celebrities, too.

The local convention bureau may be able to offer similar assistance, with a welcoming speech, perhaps, participation in the business programme or, more likely, with the social activities. The bureau may have an extensive database which you can use as well.

Signing up speakers

Next, you must approach prospective speakers in order to commission them – perhaps the hardest task of all. There is much to think about once you have reached this stage in the proceedings.

What will make speakers want to attend your conference? Should you try to identify their motives, so that you can work on these later?

Will just being there make them feel important? Will they enjoy speaking to delegates and be flattered by the attention and interest in what they have to say? (This is probably why the managing director wants to talk!)

Is it money that will appeal to them – a substantial fee backed up by generous travel and accommodation allowances, miscellaneous extras, unlimited use of the hotel's facilities and services and a choice of gifts from your range of products?

There may be other motives such as the chance to visit an exotic location, to stay in a luxurious hotel, the opportunity to meet friends again, renew business acquaintances, and make new friends or establish business contacts.

How should you approach these selected speakers?

Face-to-face contact has the advantage of informality and gives you the chance to explain, answer questions and persuade. The disadvantages are that it may be too informal for some speakers who may construe this type of approach as rather forward or even demanding. The pros and cons of a telephone approach are much the same as a face-to-face contact, but may also incur other disadvantages, such as difficulty in judging a mood by voice alone and the inability to show supporting materials.

A more sensible approach might be to write a letter. The benefits of this more formal method include the opportunity to think about what you want to state, how to phrase it correctly, and whether to include explanatory documents. The drawbacks include the possibility of a poorly phrased letter, misinterpretations and misunderstanding.

It may be wise to use an intermediary. This has the advantage that the go-between will know the potential speaker well and can time and phrase their approach accordingly, but also carries the risk that the intermediary may not put across your message in the way that you want them to do.

What needs to be discussed with each speaker at this early stage?

The conference   Its type, theme, purpose, the audience, provisional business and social activities, dates, location. Cover as much *relevant* information as possible but keep it brief and to the point, bearing in mind what the speaker wants and needs to know.

The speaker's role   What do you want them to do? Arrive at a certain hour? Make a speech on a particular topic, for a given length of time? Take any questions from the floor, as appropriate? Do you want the speaker to join the delegates for lunch and present an award to the top salesperson, to be around to participate in the fun and games during the afternoon and/or depart at a specified time?

Your offer   The fee, if relevant. This will probably be reached by negotiation. Travel and accommodation arrangements – their responsibility or your responsibility? Clarify whether or not the speaker is bringing a partner and, if they are, whether he or she is staying over. Who is responsible? Who is paying – including miscellaneous expenses and sundry extras? Specify what's what, now!

Anything else?   Are there any other details relevant to your individual situation which need to be covered? Be prepared to negotiate at all times, perhaps to meet on several occasions, talk regularly on the telephone and exchange letters up to and on agreement.

What should happen after you have (eventually) reached agreement with all the speakers?

Confirm everything in writing   Conference location? Dates? Times? Business and social activities? Speakers' commitments? Lengths of stay? Obligations while there? Financial and other arrangements – fees, payment dates, travel and accommodation data? Parties to sign and date on verification of agreements? Miscellaneous other matters?

Obtain details from the speakers   Photographs? Biographical notes for use in mailshots to would-be delegates, press releases and general advertising? Synopses of their speeches for your suggestions and/or approval? Lists of any supporting equipment needed, such as flip-charts or slide projector and screen, so you can make arrangements?

Finalize the programme Notify speakers and draw their attention to any amendments? Confirm the contents of speeches and use of equipment and so on in the light of any changes? Provide any documents and materials relating to the conference such as sales reports and trade newsletters, which may be of value or interest to them?

What else? Check that all is well on a regular, ongoing basis and follow up any queries, concerns and worries. Attend to travel and accommodation arrangements early on. Book equipment at the earliest opportunity. Meet in rehearsals. Make changes, as necessary. Get speakers to the event, relaxed and on time and make sure they are happy with their accommodation and so forth.

Is that all? No! You should have reserves lined up just in case any of your first-choice speakers drops out prior to the conference. You and/or your colleagues should be prepared to step in at the last moment if speakers are taken ill at the event.

Recommended reading

Cochrane, P. (1993), *The Power of the Phone*, Pitman, London.
Goldmann, H. (1995), *How to Communicate and Win People*, Pitman, London.
Taylor, J. (1994), *Successful Telephone Techniques*, Kogan Page, London.

7

Inviting Delegates

Think carefully about the delegates you would like to come to your conference. Take care in picking suitable delegates, drawing up a contacts list and approaching people successfully in order to persuade them to attend the event.

Picking suitable delegates

Not surprisingly, you must begin by deciding exactly who you want to participate in your conference. The following questions will enable you to identify those people who should be invited to the event.

In general terms, who do you want to attend the conference?

People who will benefit from the business and social activities by being rewarded through reaching a trade agreement, by learning how to use a new product properly, or by re-establishing or making new contacts? Those who will help you achieve your goals by being motivated, buying goods or promoting revamped services?

Others who need to be invited for political purposes, such as colleagues, associates, those whom colleagues and associates want to invite and people who feel they ought to be there? Ought you to invite such people to be polite, to keep the peace or stay popular with your boss?

Be prepared to invite anyone else who should attend.

More specifically, what particular factors will affect your choice of delegates?

The type of event you are staging may influence your choice. If it is a trade conference should you invite everyone in the trade association? If not, which ones? If it is a training event should you invite key members of staff who need to master a new skill or all your employees?

The subjects you intend to incorporate in the programme have an influence. For example, your trade event could include a discussion designed to reach an outline agreement on a new code of conduct for members and this might imply that it would be worthwhile having media representatives there to convey the news to the outside world.

Your objectives are a factor, too. What are they – to reward, motivate, take orders, make sales, obtain free publicity, discuss the marketplace, demonstrate goods, or a mixture of these?

Can you think of any other factors which you need to take into account in your particular circumstances? If so, note them down.

How many delegates should be invited to your conference?

A selected few, just the top salespeople perhaps, the best or the élite – is that wise? Perhaps all the sales team – in-house and outsiders, the most successful, the least successful? Should you invite everyone and anybody? What is most sensible?

What should be the main influences on your decision regarding the number of delegates to invite?

The purpose of the event is a major influence on your decision. Is it to reward the best of the sales team and to motivate others to do better, or to review everyone's sales results and set company-wide targets for the whole salesforce?

Another factor is the budget available to you. Are delegates paying their own way – and their partners too? How much have you set aside to pay for delegates and partners, their travel, accommodation and any extras? What will happen if you exceed these limits? Can you balance it out elsewhere and, if so, what will be the effects of these cutbacks?

Are you free to select your delegates?

If so, review all these questions, answer them fully and piece together a clear understanding of the type and number of delegates required. Do you know who in particular you wish to invite?

If not, perhaps you have been told to invite certain people and not others by the managing director or someone else. Can you still invite additional delegates though – those who will benefit both themselves and your firm by attending, and so on?

Drawing up a contacts list

Having identified who you are looking for in terms of types and numbers, go on to compile a list of people who are worth approaching. This list may be drawn from a variety of sources, as follows.

Will they be from inside your organization?

You   Would you benefit from being a delegate? Don't forget that you may learn something from a speech, a discussion, an examination of a new product, or whatever. Shouldn't you also participate if this is so?

Your close colleagues   Are they going to attend, and for the right reasons – not because it is a 'beanfeast', a 'good skive', and so forth? Can they put you in touch with other, suitable delegates?

Other people within the firm   Purchasing? Production? Marketing? Sales? Finance? Personnel? Part-timers? Full-timers? Temporary staff? Juniors? Senior employees? Directors? Do they know of others who should be there?

Will they be from outside your organization?

Should business associates, your suppliers, sellers, intermediaries, your customers and others be there? Are they aware of other people who should also attend?

Other contacts such as friends and relatives are unlikely to be invited, but are they aware of others who could be ideal delegates in the circumstances?

Have you thought about the sponsors of your conference, if appropriate?

Your trade body   Should representatives of your trade body be invited and/or their members? Can it provide you with its membership list?

Training and Enterprise Council   Should you invite key members of their team or ask them for a contacts list of would-be delegates?

Department of Trade and Industry   Perhaps representatives of the regional offices may wish to come along or might have mailing lists which you could use?

Other firms involved with the conference   Perhaps those holding an exhibition alongside your event? Do you want their key personnel to attend? Could they supply you with a list of their clients?

Are there any other individuals or organizations to consider?

The local tourist board may be able to suggest names to be added to your growing list of prospective delegates. The nearby convention bureau may also help.

Approaching delegates

With your composite list now completed, move on to approach possible delegates, in order to persuade them to attend your conference – not always the easiest of tasks! Several decisions need to be made at this stage in the process.

Why will delegates come to the event? Is it wise to recognize their reasons for attending so that you can build on them?

Your firm's reputation may be the motivating factor. Is it a market leader of considerable prestige whose views and activities are widely held to be significant?

The subject matter could be the draw. Is it a hot topic, a 'must-know' matter? Will people want to be there so that they do not miss out on essential information and advice?

Are the speakers the attraction – the opportunity to hear an interesting speech, meet an admired person, see that celebrity and talk to that personality?

Are in-house delegates attending because they have been told to come along by their heads of department? Are external delegates being sent along by their companies whether they like it or not? You should try to interest and motivate them nonetheless.

Do delegates have other reasons for coming, such as the opportunity to travel to an unusual place, to spend time in a first-class hotel, to get together with old friends, to make new ones, to socialize with existing and new business contacts – or a combination of these different reasons?

What is the best way to invite these delegates to the conference?

Should you or one of your colleagues approach them personally? This might be a suitable strategy if you know them well and want the opportunity to chat informally, answer questions and so on. It may not be appropriate when dealing with people who might not welcome an informal approach and could even be annoyed or offended by it.

Telephone invitations have the advantage of being informal and allowing instant, two-way communication. The disadvantages are that you might call at an inconvenient moment or find it hard to judge the person you speak to by their voice.

Should you send a letter of invitation? This might be most appropriate when you wish to incorporate persuasive, back-up documents but inappropriate if you are not sure how to phrase an invitation.

You could issue invitations via a third party. A business associate might be better placed to invite delegates on your behalf if he or she knows them well and understands what makes them tick. Will he or she approach them properly, though, and say what you want them to?

What information needs to be given to delegates at this point?

Some details about this conference – the type, theme, purpose, speakers, planned business and social programmes, dates, location. What else can you think of that delegates both want and need to know? (Keep it brief and relevant, though!)

Data on the benefits for delegates – why they should attend, how they will enjoy it, what they will gain from coming to the event. Should this be the central focus of your message? Almost certainly yes. Everyone wants to know what is in this for them.

Some facts and figures – fees, if appropriate, for delegates and their partners. What will they receive in return? Who is responsible for making travel and accommodation arrangements? Make clear who will be responsible for expenses, especially if the delegate is bringing his or her partner.

Have you overlooked something obvious which delegates need to know about – arrival times, departure times, something which appears relatively minor but which needs to be clarified now? Who is paying for the telephone and drinks bill?

What happens after they have accepted your invitation to the event?

Confirm key details in writing (if you have not already done so) including location, dates, times, business and social activities, fees and payment dates, travel and accommodation arrangements and any other miscellaneous arrangements that you can think of.

Ask delegates to register well in advance so that you can estimate numbers, names, companies, addresses, telephone and fax numbers, attendance details, arrival dates, departure dates, fees for attending some activities and not others perhaps, accommodation requests and payment arrangements.

Finalize the conference programme and inform delegates of any changes. Supply any documents and materials which may be of use or interest to them, such as new product literature and press releases.

Check to see if you should attend to anything else. Are there any questions or uncertainties? Is something unclear? Should you make travel and accommodation arrangements as early as possible and any amendments, as necessary? Is everything organized to get them to the conference on time, fresh and relaxed, and ensure they are happy with their accommodation? Are you ready to begin the business programme?

Recommended reading

Bartram, P. (1994), *Perfect Business Writing*, Random House, London.
Bird, P. (1994), *Tame That Phone!*, Pitman, London.
Forsyth, P. (1993), *Agreed!*, Kogan Page, London.
Heymes, P. (1990), *How to Perfect Your Selling Skills*, Kogan Page, London.

8

Publicizing Your Conference

Once you have commissioned speakers and invited delegates to the conference you can think about promoting the event further afield. Perhaps you want to attract additional, as yet unknown, speakers and delegates and some form of promotional campaign can enable you to make contact and encourage them to come forward. It is just as likely that you simply want to generate good publicity for your firm and announcing that a promotional event is being staged to launch new products or a training day is being held to update staff will help to convey a positive image of your organization. Probably the most common ways of promoting a conference are to issue press releases, mail out letters and advertise in the press.

Issuing press releases

One of your first promotional actions may be to draft a press release to be sent to appropriate media contacts who can help to publicize your business and the conference.

What is a press release? What are the advantages and disadvantages of issuing them?

A press release is a one- or two-page statement outlining a recent or forthcoming news event which is forwarded to selected media contacts in anticipation of free publicity for that event and to the individuals and organizations involved with it. The types of 'news event' that might be covered in a press release are the addition of a new director to the board, the opening of another shop, office or factory and the staging of a first-class conference.

What are the key advantages of using press releases to publicize your event? There is minimal expense involved – they cost you virtually nothing, just your time plus some stationery and stamps, and are certainly much cheaper than other forms of promotion, such as press advertising. They are also flexible – it is up to you what to include, how to state it, how long you take to state it, when you send them and where you send them. So there is very little, if anything, to be lost by issuing them.

Their main disadvantages are that they are hard to write well. Typically they are full of gaps (so when exactly does that conference start?), contain irrelevant material (what does the chairman's life history have to do with the event?), can ramble on and on (so what's the point of it?), and the response is unpredictable. There is an element of pot luck involved here. Will the recipient be interested? Will there be space to publish an article? Will it be printed when you want it to be. The answer is often 'no, no and no'!

Should you use press releases as part of your promotional activities? What are the key influences on your choice?

Your audience or prospective speakers, perhaps. Are you still seeking a 'draw' to pull in delegates? Are you short of numbers, not yet having attracted enough to guarantee a profit? Do you need more influential organizations and individuals who can convey a quality image of your firm and event? Who do you want to attract – what type of organization (numbers, sizes, locations, activities)? What sort of individuals (numbers, sexes, ages, occupations, interests, locations)? Just who are you trying to reach?

Which media do your target audience see, hear and read – television, radio, the press? More specifically, which particular media are they most likely to come into contact with – which specific television station, radio station, newspaper and magazine. Just as important, which ones might be interested in receiving a release and running a feature – television perhaps (fairly unlikely), radio (probably not), newspapers, magazines (more hopeful)?

Does the purpose and theme of your event make it newsworthy? Almost certainly not if it is an incentive event to reward and motivate your best salespeople. Probably yes if it is a trade conference held to discuss and agree on new guidelines for the industry. Can you think of anything else which might make the event newsworthy, such as its location if it is held on board a ship, in a theme park or in another unusual place. Is this likely to interest whoever receives the press release?

Minimal cost is involved in issuing a press release – a little time and effort, stationery, stamps and the cost of faxing them through at most. So can you afford to use them? (Definitely.) Do they offer you value for money? (Certainly. They do not bite into your budget as other forms of promotional activity will do. Overspending elsewhere can even be balanced out by the lower-than-expected cost of a publicity campaign consisting mainly of press releases.)

What should your press release look like? What should be included in it?

Figure 8.1 on page 108 is an example of a press release. See if yours fulfils the following criteria.

Appearance   Use top-notch, letterheaded paper. You work for a classy firm and this is an important conference, so be stylish (it is expensive, but worthwhile). Use A4 paper (big enough to be noticed) and write the release on one or two sides. A5 paper is too small, too cramped, too cheap and second rate.

Layout   'Press release' at the top? An eye-catching heading, perhaps to the left? Date in the top right corner? The first paragraph must have impact to keep them reading. Have subsequent paragraphs of the 'who–what–when–where–why–how' variety. Put 'more' at the bottom of the first page and the heading plus '. . . 2' at the top left side of the second. Then go on! State 'ends' at the end of the release and add a name and telephone and fax numbers in case the recipient wants further information.

Contents   Basic details about the conference – its type, theme, purpose, dates, times, location, business activities, social activities even, and perhaps fees. What else? Include the benefits of attending so far as the delegates are concerned? The experts who will be there, ready and willing to pass on their knowledge and expertise and the interesting celebrities to be met? Anything else?

Style   Brisk and business-like – you're dealing with busy, hard-nosed

Press Information

Release date: 1 November 1994

The
MARKETING
GUILD

Attention: Diary/News Editor

The Marketing Guild Conference, Thurs 19 January 1995, Holiday Inn, London-Heathrow. 9am - 5pm. £195+VAT.

From The Marketing Guild, 1 Houghton Court, Houghton Regis, Beds LU5 5DY. 01582 861556.

A new one-day workshop to help business owners gain more profitable customers on a limited marketing budget is the Marketing Guild Conference from the Marketing Guild, on Thurs 19 Jan 1995 at the Holiday Inn-London Heathrow, at £195+VAT.

It gives ample hands-on experience in creating effective ads, brochures and direct mail, and includes a free critique of delegates' own materials.

Designed for the business professional who is not a marketing expert, the day promises over 200 fresh ideas to win more and better sales leads, and convert them to profitable sale.

The Marketing Guild is an association of 1200 business owners. Over 12,000 delegates have attended its 200 UK conferences to date.

Details from: The Marketing Guild Ltd, 1 Houghton Court, Houghton Regis, Beds LU5 5DY. 0582 861556. Fax 0582 864913.

Editor: (1) You are welcome to attend and review any Guild event. Please contact us for a press pass. Editorial contacts: Julie Rogers or Nick Robinson, 0582 861556.

(2) Conference brochure enclosed.

Figure 8.1   Press release

journalists here! Have it typed in double-spacing with wide margins and leave plenty of room for their notes and amendments. The text should be short and concise, with specific, informative paragraphs, easy-to-understand language and quotes to liven it up perhaps and to add credibility. Avoid hype and flannel, though. Don't capitalize parts of the text; underline or put them in italics – make sure it is simple to read.

Having written a press release, what should you do with it?

Decide exactly where it should be sent – those publications which are read by your audience! Do you know which ones these are? It may be your professional association's magazine if you are staging a trade conference, fellow concerns' or in-house journals if you are holding a training event. If you are not sure, look at *British Rate and Data* (BRAD), a 600-page directory that lists all the main UK publications (see 'Reference Tools', page 215). Find it in your local library. Make your choice!

Decide when your press release should be issued. When do you want the event to be publicized? How often? Six months, three months and one week before it is staged to attract speakers, then delegates and finally last-minute delegates, as appropriate? Can you therefore prepare three versions of your release, each with a twist, another angle, something to ensure second and third mentions? How long do you want a feature to run? Perhaps one month is appropriate for a professional association's magazine, three months in a fellow concern's in-house journal? What is best for you?

Post your press release at the relevant time, marked for the attention of the news editor. Put the editor's name, rather than 'The News Editor'. This is a release written for him or her alone, not a mass circular (even though it probably is)! Refer to BRAD for this information – telephoning the chosen publication to confirm and check the spelling (get it absolutely correct). For speed and a classier image, fax that release. Then keep your fingers crossed.

Be available if the news editor or a reporter wants to follow up the release for further information, more details or to arrange for photographs to be taken – perhaps of the new product you are launching. Keep track of the responses to your press release. Do you now have a useful media contacts list? Note who ran a feature, whether it was a positive one, what the effects were and who and how many enquired as a result of it. Which would-be delegates registered and in what numbers? What have you learned for the future?

Mailing letters

Direct mail is another option available to conference organizers seeking to publicize their event to the outside world, whether they want to attract more people to attend it or simply to boost their overall image.

What is direct mail? What are the pros and cons of adopting this approach?

Direct mail is personalized messages sent to named contacts, either at work or at home. Business-to-business mail comprises mailshots sent to fellow business concerns; consumer mail is delivered to members of the public at home. Whatever its type, it usually consists of an envelope, a letter and various inserts such as a reply-paid postcard and a registration form – all addressed to a specific person. It is this personalization which distinguishes it from unnamed and unaddressed junk mail.

Its advantages include its versatility in addressing businesses or the public at work or at home, countrywide. You can reach ten people or even tens of thousands when you want and include whatever you wish. Direct mail is targetable, enabling you to put across your message to a very precise, identified audience. It is very personal, too (one-to-one contact is rather flattering). You can monitor how many were sent out, when, where, how many and who replied. It is often also cost effective – usually far more so than advertising in other media such as the press.

Disadvantages include the time it takes to prepare for and run a winning campaign, build a suitable contacts list from in-house and/or external sources, check that it is up to date and accurate and select the right approach and contents. Sending them out, monitoring responses and so on also take time. The fact that it is a highly specialized medium which, to be successful, requires knowledge and skills to produce an eyecatching envelope, a persuasive letter or supportive inserts may also be a drawback.

Should you include direct mail in your publicity campaign? What most affects your decision?

The target audience   Those prospective speakers you are still looking to attract? The would-be delegates you want to register as soon as possible? Those influential organizations and individuals you are seeking to impress? Do you know precisely who they are? If not, can you find out by talking to colleagues and contacting associations? Equally significant, do you know exactly where they are? If not, can you discover their specific whereabouts from your files or from outside publications? (Unless you know who and where your audience is, you cannot use direct mail!)

The medium   Does it allow you to publicize your firm and the event when you want – to the day, if you post mail, to the minute, if you fax that letter? Can you advertise as often as you wish, once only if you like, several times, even endlessly, if you prefer? Does direct mail enable you to promote the event for as long as you require – in a short, sharp burst over three or four weeks, perhaps, or a longer, steadier campaign over several months?

The conference   What type of event are you staging? What is its main purpose and theme? Is it ideally suited to direct mail activities, to writing a persuasive, 'come-and-see' letter? Don't ignore the fact that it might not be. Recipients may need to be persuaded to attend a promotional conference, but it is less likely for an incentive event.

The costs incurred   Is this a costly medium? Yes! It can be expensive and time-consuming to build a mailing list, keep it up to date and accurate, provide envelopes, letters, reply devices and other inserts such as gifts. Mailing out, monitoring the response rate and so on is also expensive. Can you afford it? Does it offer value for money? If the returns are substantial and relevant, it does; if they are limited and less relevant, maybe not.

What types of envelope should you pick for your mailshots? What should they look like?

Plain manilla envelopes are inexpensive but rather drab and nondescript. Coloured ones are more expensive but do attract attention. Window envelopes, although more expensive, are convenient and time-saving as the name and address can show through and you don't need sticky labels. Those without windows are cheaper, although they take time to be addressed. How about an eyecatching logo or a puzzling slogan rubber stamped or printed to intrigue and to encourage the recipient to open it now?

What else should you consider with regard to envelopes? Pick good quality rather than the cheapest ones (this is a first-class conference, not a second-rate one). Make sure that they are large and strong

---

NEW SERIES!

"I haven't a clue
what to do for a new
promotional idea to
build my business"

"No problem. Why not
come along to a Guild
mini-conference - and
pick up *dozens* of ideas?"

For the personal attention of:
Mr I Maitland
5 Thomas Avenue
Trimley St Mary
Suffolk
IP10 0YS   ON2

Dear Mr Maitland

Your invitation to acquire dozens of fresh,
practical ways to win new business NOW...

Winning more business, more profitably calls - not just for
selling harder - but for marketing smarter. Let us give you
dozens of great marketing ideas at once, in this NEW series of
conferences. They're daring, oddball - you won't find them in
textbooks - but they work.

Every one can bring your service business new clients and new
profits. They'll become yours, without obligation, to use in
your business the very next day.

We are offering you this idea-packed 100-minute presentation
for just £29.95 + VAT, exactly what it costs us to mount it, with
no strings then or later. Because we want you to sample the
Marketing Guild. To explore its ideas and services, and prove for
yourself how they can help you win more client business.

Every idea you'll hear is taken from a recent Guild newsletter,
report or seminar. Our members gain more than 1000 such ideas every
year when they join, plus unlimited and direct access to all the
Guild's profit-winning information, plus... but we'll tell you more
when you accept our invitation!

**The mini-conference is at a venue close to you. Registration is
from 2pm for a prompt 2.30pm start, end around 4.30pm.**

Whether or not you choose to join the Guild, you'll come away
with dozens of sparkling new practical ideas to use in your service
business at once. Please send or fax back the RSVP as soon as
possible to reserve your place.

Yours sincerely

Julie Rogers

JULIE ROGERS
Marketing Director

PS: We **guarantee** that your small investment will be returned many,
many times when you practise these ideas. If for any reason, you
disagree, having paid and attended, **we will refund your payment in
full,** cheerfully and without question!

1 Houghton Court	**The MARKETING GUILD**	HelpLine: 0582 861556
Houghton Regis		Fax: 0582 864913
LU5 5DY, Beds		The Marketing Guild Ltd

002453

Figure 8.2   Mailshot letter

enough to carry all the enclosures and they are accurate, neat and clean, with correct and carefully placed details. Should the details be handwritten or typed? Handwritten details are personalized but time-consuming and uneconomic for larger mailings. Typing? – the reverse! Is stamped or franked more personal? Which is more time effective? Whatever you decide, be practical.

How about the letter and its appearance, layout, contents and style?

Figure 8.2 gives an example of a letter; see if it meets these criteria:

Appearance Use quality paper which, preferably, matches the envelope. Watermarked sheets are another possibility – but although they look classy they are expensive for mass mailings. Make sure that the sheets are large enough for you to complete your letter on one or two sides – if the letter is much longer than that readers will probably lose interest, if they read it at all! A4 size paper is probably the best and most popular option. For very brief letters, A5 paper may be suitable, although you still run the risk of the letter looking cramped.

Layout Use a letterhead across the top of the page, including your firm's name, address, telephone and fax numbers, and perhaps a logo. Consider using a reference number near the left margin below so that you can check and assess responses. Including the date will make the letter seem fresh, and the addition of the recipient's name and address lends a personal touch. Give thought to the style of greeting you wish to use – do you prefer the formal 'Dear Mr Hewlett' or 'Dear Robert' or something else? How do you wish to sign off? 'Yours sincerely', 'Best regards' or even 'Kind regards'? Make sure that your signature is clear and readable, with your name and title typed below it. Add 'encs' for enclosures if relevant.

Content Give straightforward information about the event. Don't overlook the basic facts! Have you detailed the type of conference, its theme and purpose, dates, times and location? Have you included an outline of the business and social programmes and the fees, if applicable? Too many mailshot letters omit some of these key points of information. Set out, also, the reasons why the recipient should attend. What is in it for them? Can they learn something new, make useful contacts or stay in a pleasant environment? Are there other good reasons why they should come along?

Style   The letter should immediately seize the reader's attention. How can this be achieved? Perhaps by turning the principal benefit into a headline, a question or slogan to make the recipient read on? Can it then convert this attention into interest and desire – to speak at, attend or promote the event – by elaborating on the key benefit in the first paragraph and explaining other benefits, backed up by independent testimony or research findings, in subsequent ones? Can you encourage the recipient to act by giving a time limit, providing a contact number and telephone and fax numbers? Encourage him or her to get in touch quickly – now!

Anything else?   Write personally – you're addressing one particular person, not a crowd. Be friendly. Talk to, not at or down to, the reader – you're equals! Write naturally, as if you were talking to him or her face-to-face. Make it easy to read, using clear, concise words and short sentences and paragraphs. Give it life and variety by including positive, enthusiastic language. You can indent paragraphs, vary widths and lengths, capitalize or underline the benefits. Consider using subheadings and bullet points to break up text. Make it an exciting read!

What about the inserts? Most notably, some sort of reply device? Other inserts? Gifts?

Examples of reply devices are shown in Figure 8.3 on pages 116–119. Figure 8.4 on page 120 is a list of gifts, some of which could be sent at this stage.

Should you enclose a reply device for requesting further details or returning a (built-in) registration form? This is courteous and encourages a response by making it easier to reply. It also guarantees that responses are made to the right address. So what should you provide? Typically, a pre-addressed postcard or envelope, either stamped, reply paid or freepost. This gives the advantage of a larger and faster response but the disadvantage that you may receive replies from half-hearted readers who would not otherwise have responded. This will incur extra costs as well.

What else do you need to know about the reply device? You should make sure it is easy to complete, can be written on in biro and is not too glossy for a felt-tipped pen. Ensure that any instructions are clear and simple to understand and it is straightforward enough to fill out. Are the questions concise and unambiguous and is there plenty of room for the answers? Can you complete as many details as possible for them? (It all helps!)

Can other inserts be included? A registration form, perhaps – part of, or attached to, the reply device? A product sample maybe? It's difficult to ignore a mysterious shape, and people like to receive a free gift to examine at their leisure. Freebies can be costly, however. They need larger, stronger envelopes and take time to package. Gifts also need to be tasteful and interesting; otherwise they may damage your credibility by cheapening your image. Do you want to include sales literature, such as a product catalogue? Or explanatory, illustrated brochures and leaflets for people to mull over? They are expensive, though, and carry the risk of overkill. If you send too much information, people may see no point in attending the actual event!

Once you have composed your mailshot, what should you do next?

Decide exactly who you want to receive your mailings. If you do not know already, build up a mailing list of names and addresses from in-house, using enquiry forms, membership and subscription files, sales and accounts records and product guarantee forms. Useful outside sources are yearbooks, journals, directories and even electoral registers. Selective mailing lists can also be hired or purchased from professional bodies, such as chambers of commerce, clubs and societies, and specialist mailing list companies.

Make sure that you obtain your information from reputable sources and that they, in turn, have acquired it in an honest and reliable manner. For example, are your mailing list suppliers all members of the Direct Marketing Association (UK) Ltd or the Direct Mail Services Standards Board? Do they abide by the guidelines set down by these bodies? See 'Useful Contacts', page 219.

Check also that your list covers your target market and that it is accurate and up to date. How old is the information, how was it recorded, how frequently is it checked and by what means? Keep your own lists up to date too, by referring to membership renewal forms or the next yearbook, perhaps.

Finalize a timetable for your mailings early on so that speakers can be signed up promptly and delegates can be registered at the earliest opportunity. How many mailshots do you need to send? Three is probably sufficient – if the recipients have not responded by the third letter, they probably never will. Can you compose three different letters, each more persuasive than the last? At what time intervals should you send them? Three to six weeks apart, or less than that? This may be a demanding schedule but, if it is any longer, people may lose interest.

Practical sales promotion

Just £29.95 + VAT

Acquire dozens of fresh, ready-to-go ways to win new sales for your service business NOW -

...in this highly acclaimed Marketing Mini-Conference, an ultra-intensive two-hour introduction to the Marketing Guild

What you will hear:

- Four novel **sales promotion** ideas - that cost next to nothing - but which invariably bring you more clients.

- Four clever ways to use **direct marketing** more profitably - including an actual example of a letter that typically pulls an amazing 85% response.
    Plus a way to mail the private mailing list of even your fiercest competitor - with your competitor's warm approval!

- Six little-known strategies for making your **advertising** work harder...

Including how to book your advertising at up to 80% below rate card in prime media every time (even how to negotiate "free" display ads).

- Four bright techniques for **converting enquiries** into major sales - even over a very long sales cycle. Even when you think you've lost the sale.

- Three stunningly simple, but little practised, ways to build more and bigger business with your **existing customers** at once - you can try them while you listen! *See over...*

Registration from 2pm. Starts 2.30pm. Finishes approx. 4.30pm.

Tue 23rd Aug 1994: Holiday Inn, **LONDON-HEATHROW**

Wed 31st Aug 1994: Garden House Hotel, **CAMBRIDGE**

Wed 7th Sept 1994: Novotel, **COVENTRY**

Tue 13th Sept 1994: Forte Crest, **MANCHESTER airport**

Thur 15th Sept 1994: Hilton National, Garforth, **LEEDS**

Fee £29.95 + VAT (£35.19). Close to motorways. Free parking. Map provided

YOUR TOTAL GUARANTEE: We pledge that your small investment *will* be quickly returned many, many times when you practise the ideas outlined. *Or* else we will refund your payment upon demand, in full, cheerfully and without question.

Figure 8.3   Reply devices

Examine dozens of "breakthrough" ideas that have *already* brought new profits for these companies...

A **marketing services agency** attracted 50% more visitors - of better quality - to its sales reception. *How?* By adding just one extra sentence to its invitation - and we reveal it!

An **office equipment firm** attracted hundreds of top buyers to its modest exhibition stand, on a fraction of its rivals' budgets, while their stands stood empty. Hear no fewer than four different ways you can adapt this idea, whether you sell to secretaries, technicians, fleet managers, professional buyers or customers of *any* kind - even City bankers!

A **corporate gifts company** won 150% more response from its mailings to Board directors, using the same letter to the same list, by making just one simple change to the package. We show you how to do likewise, whoever you're mailing and whatever you're marketing...

An **electrical distributor** picked up top accounts from blue chip customers, kept their loyalty *and* maintained premium prices during severe recession - while his competitors frantically cut prices to survive. You can use his innovative idea to keep and grow clients, whoever your clients are. *Proof?* Even **solicitors** adapted it, to market legal services - with the full approval of the Law Society!

...and discover precisely how *you* can use them in your business too!

A **financial services firm** applied three breathtakingly simple tactics, costing virtually nothing, to keep its prospects "warm" over a period of many months until they were ready to buy. You can employ them in *your* company, whether or not you have a long "sales cycle".

Figure 8.3   Reply devices (continued)

What they told us

"One method recommended was used in my capacity as Sales Manager with Legal Protection Group, a subsidiary of Sun Alliance. This idea contributed towards an almost unbelievable response of 64%. I have appointments and group seminars booked up to three months ahead from one mailing." Martin Gover, Managing Director, Selclene.

"Thanks for the innovative ideas [which we] use at the prospecting stage in our contract recruitment business." Nick Gill, Managing Director, Reflex Recruitment Services.

"Just one idea picked up from attending the mini-conference smoothed the way to us obtaining a client whose annual audit fee is more than eighty times the cost of the conference." David Moncur, Partner, Scott Oswald & Co, Chartered Accountants.

"By combining three different ideas... I achieved a massive 14% response rate in the IBM mainframe software market, some of which have already purchased software... the average is 2%. " Chris Williams, Sales Manager, Interactive Computing Europe.

"Thought-provoking and of great practical use," Bernard Stewart-Deane, Bidwells Estate Agents.

Who will benefit

Directors, owners, partners and principals of service companies selling to businesses, who have personal authority to make strategic marketing decisions. It is NOT suitable for staff less senior than this.

A little about us

The Marketing Guild is dedicated to helping professional and creative service companies gain more from their business assets, through the astute use of unconventional marketing ideas. Established in 1987, it is an international network of business directors and marketing professionals. It publishes the practical newsletter Strategic Marketing. It innovates seminars, reports and resource materials, and facilitates joint venturing among its many thousands of members and delegates. These range from marketing agencies to legal and financial services, from management and technical consultants to manufacturers and resellers. From start-up firms to market leaders.

To enrol in the mini-conference

Simply complete and return the invitation enclosed with your cheque (payable to The Marketing Guild Ltd) or credit card payment for £35.19 (£29.95 + VAT). Credit card acceptances may be faxed: 0582 864913. Your joining instructions are sent with a VAT receipt and map. If you cannot attend, audio cassette recordings of the mini-conference may be purchased separately at £59.50+VAT (£69.91).

The Marketing Guild Ltd, 1 Houghton Court, Houghton Regis, Beds LU5 5DY. Helpline: 0582 861556

Please make payment with booking. We regret that no person can be allowed entrance to the Mini-Conference unless payment has been received.
Bankers: Midland Bank, King St., Luton. Reg. office: 29 Cardiff Rd., Luton LU1 1PP. Reg no: 2155404

DN

Figure 8.3   Reply devices (continued)

```
                                              ┌──────────────┐
                                              │  No stamp    │
                                              │  required    │
                                              │  if posted   │
                                              │  in UK       │
                                              └──────────────┘



    The Marketing Guild Ltd
    FREEPOST LOL 2052
    1 Houghton Court,
    Houghton Regis
    Beds LU5 5UX
    England
```

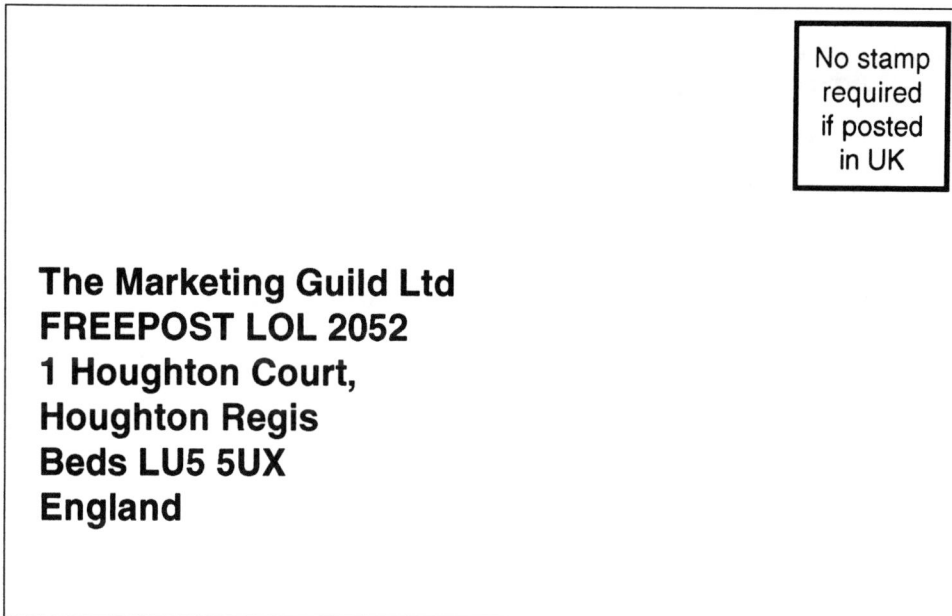

Figure 8.3   Reply devices (concluded)

Post your mailshots at the scheduled times and monitor the responses to them. This is a relatively easy task. Simply record the number of mailshots sent, how many and which recipients replied, how many enquiries led to registrations and who they were. To check whether you have obtained value for money from this costly process, calculate also the cost per enquiry received and the cost per actual registration. Did you obtain enough registrations to make a profit? Did you break even? Will you make any changes for the future?

Advertising in the press

You will almost certainly also consider advertising generally, most likely in the press – an all-embracing term which encompasses a wide and extremely diverse range of newspapers, magazines and other miscellaneous publications.

How wide and diverse is the range of press publications?

The range of newspapers spans national dailies and Sundays, regional dailies, Sundays, weeklies, bi-weeklies and free weeklies. They all have widely differing approaches to news coverage and reporting, and

☐ Address book		☐ Magnifier	
☐ Advertising bag		☐ Manicure set	
		☐ Memo pad	
☐ Badge		☐ Money clip	
☐ Balloon			
☐ Baseball cap		☐ Notebook	
☐ Blotter		☐ Notepad	
☐ Block pad			
☐ Bookmark		☐ Paper clip dispenser	
☐ Bottle opener		☐ Paper clips	
☐ Business card case		☐ Pen	
☐ Business card file		☐ Penlight	
		☐ Pen stand	
☐ Calculator		☐ Pencil	
☐ Calendar		☐ Pencil sharpener	
☐ Carrier bag		☐ Personal organizer	
☐ Chequebook case		☐ Picture frame	
☐ Coaster		☐ Planner	
☐ Coin holder		☐ Playing cards	
☐ Conference badge		☐ Post-it pad	
☐ Conference folder		☐ Post-it pad holder	
		☐ Purse	
☐ Diary			
☐ Dictionary		☐ Ruler	
☐ Flag		☐ Scarf	
		☐ Scissors	
☐ Golf calculator		☐ Shoe-shine kit	
☐ Golf card holder		☐ Spellchecker	
☐ Golf rules book		☐ Sticker	
☐ Golf tee pack			
		☐ Tape measure	
☐ Jigsaw puzzle		☐ Tax disc holder	
☐ Jotter pad		☐ Tie	
		☐ Torch	
☐ Keycase		☐ Travel clock	
☐ Keychain		☐ Travel toiletries pack	
☐ Key fob		☐ T-shirt	
☐ Keyring			
		☐ Wall planner	
☐ Letter opener			
☐ Lipstick case		And many more	
☐ Luggage tag			

Figure 8.4   Gifts: a checklist

appeal to various, definable groups of the population. They also have different circulation and pass-on readership figures and therefore markedly different advertisement rates.

The breadth of magazines available includes general interest publications of widespread and popular appeal, consumer-specific titles aimed at special interest groups and business titles related to particular products and services, to jobs and careers or to trade and industries. They all address their own mix of topics, attract assorted groups of people, have differing circulation and pass-on readership figures and, again, widely varying advertisement rates.

There are also miscellaneous publications, such as directories, year-books, in-house journals, guidebooks and even programmes, bro-chures, timetables and maps. All of these deal with varying subjects and are published for different and definable sets of organizations and individuals. As with the other groups of publications above, their advertisement rates vary according to their circulation and pass-on readership figures.

So what are the main benefits of advertising your conference in the press?

Newspaper advertising can reach a broad cross-section of a local popu-lation and/or scattered groups nationwide. You can place advertise-ments in sections or supplements where you feel they will be most effective, varying them between newspapers or editions and ensuring that they are published on a given day or in a specific week. It allows you the opportunity to be topical and offers regular, day-after-day advertising if required and at short notice if necessary.

Magazine advertising can be targeted towards well-defined groups of interested and informed people. It also carries the advantage that readers will be more likely to believe and trust your advertisement because it is in 'their' magazine. Your advertisements can be varied and placed in different publications to maximize their chances of being seen. Magazines are often read by people when they are in a leisurely, receptive mood, in more detail and possibly for longer periods of time than newspapers, and this lifespan affords an advantage in that your advertisement may be read and re-read several times. You might like to consider using colour to enhance its appeal.

Miscellaneous publications such as directories and yearbooks have the status and respectability to add credibility to your advertisements. They will be seen by a specialized and receptive group of readers who will retain the publication for some time and may therefore see your advertisement time and time again. Use specific publications to target knowledgeable and interested readers, varying the format, style and position of your displays. Don't forget to consider the use of colour too.

In-house journals have the advantage of a well-defined, identifiable readership. Your advertisements will be viewed as trustworthy and reputable because they will be perceived as being 'company-approved'. They can also be displayed in a variety of sizes, formats, colours and positions and can be adjusted at short notice if necessary.

You may also wish to consider advertising in programmes and brochures – say, for sporting fixtures. Another area well worth consideration is timetables, maps and guidebooks which lend an air of authority to advertisements, have a hands-on, involved readership, a long useful life and are used over and over again.

What are the drawbacks of advertising your event in the press?

Most newspaper readers simply will not be interested in your advertisement. Many readers who might be interested may well miss it, since few people read a newspaper from cover to cover or for any length of time. Also, their response to the advertisement may vary according to their mood at the time, which is difficult to predict, and the absence of colour may lessen its impact. Keep in mind, too, that newspapers have a short lifespan – here today and gone tomorrow!

Some magazines are published only occasionally, making it hard to build up day-to-day, week-by-week awareness. It is also impossible to predict exactly when and where the advertisement will be seen and the mood of the reader. Early copy deadlines for the submission of advertising material also make it difficult to alter the wording or format to react to changing circumstances.

It is not always possible to choose the type, content or position of advertisements in miscellaneous publications, such as directories and yearbooks. In addition, colour is rarely available, which restricts creativity. Readers tend to dip in and out of the publication and often miss advertisements, and copy has to be submitted well in advance and cannot usually be changed until the next edition – maybe a year or more later.

Some in-house journals are poorly designed, edited and printed, which may reflect badly on you. They are also not always read, or read fully, and may have a short lifespan. Pogrammes and brochures may be published only on an occasional basis and have a short span of interest for readers, being either quickly discarded or stored away. Their long copy deadlines make it difficult to remedy unsuccessful advertisements quickly. Timetables, maps and guidebooks may accommodate only restricted types and positions of advertisements. Likewise they have long deadlines, making it difficult to be topical or to make changes.

Should press advertising form part of your promotional campaign? What are the main factors that influence your decision?

Your target market Who exactly do you want to reach? It can depend on the speakers and delegates – what types of speakers and how many, what sort of delegates are coming, in what numbers and from which organizations? Which publications do they read, when, how often and for how long? If your target market is going to see your press advertisements, consider press advertising; if not, don't!

The media Which types of publication are best – newspapers, magazines or other publications? Will they enable you to advertise when you want to – probably well in advance of the conference so you have time to attract and register delegates? Will they give you the opportunity to advertise as often as you wish – occasionally or regularly so that advertisements have more likelihood of being seen? Will they allow you to promote your event for as long as you want? Long-term, steady advertising, possibly?

The event What type of conference is it? What is its purpose and theme? Which types of publication would be most appropriate? A sales conference in an in-house journal, or perhaps a trade event in the main directory of the industry? Is it really suitable for press advertising (never overlook that question!)? Does an incentive event really need to be advertised – certainly not far and wide, surely?

The costs Is press advertising expensive? (Often, yes – more than will be incurred by issuing press releases and mailing letters, anyway!) Can you afford to use the press? Does it offer value for money? (That depends on the results.) Does it give you what you want – say, another hundred or so registrations?

How should your press advertisements look? What should be incorporated in them?

Checklists for press advertisements are given in Figures 8.5 and 8.6, page 124.

Appearance What type of advertisement should you select? A display advertisement, in its own box, and perhaps set apart from others and therefore eyecatching? This will give you room to put across information and be creative, but may be costly. It may allow too much

☐   **Pick the right size of advertisement** – large enough to put in the key information but no more.

☐   **Always have a bold headline to grab the attention** – usually, the name of the conference or its message.

☐   **Use photographs, cartoons and illustrations with caution.** Keep it as clear and simple as you can.

☐   **Have an attractive typeface to persuade people to look and read on.**

☐   **Stick to the basic facts and figures** – and tell readers what's in it for them!

☐   **Use clear, easy-to-read language** – slang and jargon-free. Sound positive and upbeat too.

☐   **Choose a suitable location** – typically a special conferences section. Make sure it's seen!

☐   **Only use press advertising if you're convinced it is right for you.** Will it be seen by would-be participants?

Figure 8.5   Display advertisements: a checklist

☐   **Be wary of classifieds** – your advertisement may be hard to see amongst the others.

☐   **Use a bolder typeface for the first few words** – a 'heading' if you like – to make it stand out.

☐   **Just put over the key facts and figures** – extra words cost money!

☐   **Make sure your message is clearly understood by using plain and simple language.**

☐   **Pick the best place for your classified advertisement** – closer to the beginning than the end, and certainly not lost somewhere in the middle!

☐   **Only advertise in the press if you are totally sure it is suitable for you** – are those prospective participants going to see it? If 'no', why advertise there?

Figure 8.6   Classified advertisements: a checklist

room, perhaps, encouraging unnecessary details and highlighting creative shortcomings. A classified advertisement, then? If so, set line by line under a heading such as 'Conferences, 1996'? This will be less expensive but if there are many advertisements it could be easy to overlook.

Layout How should the advertisement be set out? With a headline to catch attention, sum up the main message and make people read on? A photograph, perhaps of a celebrity speaker? A cartoon, perhaps, or an illustration to convey or strengthen the message? Something simple, relevant and self-explanatory which is not too busy or obscure? Should the text be set in an appealing typeface to persuade people to keep reading? Do you want to use bold faces, italics or different shades – white on a black background, even? Keep it straightforward, though!

Contents What should the advertisement include? Some basic facts and figures, the type of event it is, why, where and when it is being staged, what it involves and how much it costs to come along? What else? Why readers should be there perhaps – to be part of discussions, have an input into a trade agreement or re-establish contacts with fellow trade association members? Mention what's in it for them, otherwise, they won't come!

Style Should the style have a distinctive or offbeat feel? Stick to the message and use short, to-the-point text – especially in a classified advertisement. Extra words mean more money! Use clear, understandable, jargon-free language (avoid slang). Make the text easy to read and get the facts across! Use positive words, too, and upbeat, persuasive language. Do you want readers to get in touch, perhaps to register immediately? Yes!

Position Which is the best place for it – assuming that you have a choice? Somewhere it will be seen and read most often by the right people! In general terms, should it be nearer the front than the back, alone instead of with others, at the top not the bottom of a page, to the right rather than the left, on the outside instead of the inside? More specifically, should it be in a particular section of the publication such as 'Conference News' or in a special supplement, such as 'Focus on Conferences'?

Having drafted an advertisement, how do you set about advertising in the press?

Decide which publications you want to use. If you have any ideas, contact the advertisement manager or director of each title and request a media pack, rate card and a copy of the most recent issue. If not, look in the latest edition of *British Rate and Data* (BRAD) to build up your ideas. Make your selection, then approach the appropriate advertisement managers or directors, as relevant.

Study the media pack which is a booklet setting out information about the publication. Check its price, regular columns, features, supplements, the sexes, ages, occupations, activities, interests and habits of the readership, and their opinions of the title.

Read the rate card, which is a sheet or pamphlet which lists more specific details about advertising in the publication. What are the circulation and readership figures, display advertising rates, classified advertising rates, names, telephone and extension numbers of key personnel, copy deadlines, mechanical and technical data, conditions of acceptance of advertisements and on-sale dates?

Examine your copy of the latest issue of the publication – past copies too, if you can obtain them – to gain a better understanding of editorial copy, build a fuller image of advertising copy to date and to satisfy yourself that this publication really is the right choice in your circumstances.

Decide whether or not you should advertise in this publication. Does it reach the right type of audience in the right numbers? Can you advertise when you want to and as often and for as long as you wish? Can you have the type and style of advertisement that you want, in the right position? All at an acceptable price?

Submit your advertisement to the advertisement director or manager. Be prepared to listen to his or her advice – he or she may be able to improve the advertisement by editing the contents to achieve the same message for a lower price, or by suggesting a different typeface for greater impact. He or she may also offer a better position for the same price, if one is available. Always listen to what he or she has to say.

Monitor the responses. Who and how many responded and how many of these registered, per advertisement and per publication? You can measure these easily if you place a 'key' – or identifying mark – into each advertisement. For example, in one advertisement readers are asked to telephone you; in another, a colleague. Or they may be asked to write to Department 1a for one advertisement and to 1b for the next, and so on. You can then work out which advertisement represents value for money on the basis of price of advertisement divided by number of enquiries which equals the cost per enquiry. Dividing this by the number of registrations gives you the cost per registration. Have you learned anything for next time?

Recommended reading

Bartram, P. (1995), *How to Write a Press Release*, How To Books, Plymouth.
Maitland, I. (1996), *How to Plan Direct Mail*, Cassell, London.
Maitland, I. (1996), *How to Plan Press Advertising*, Cassell, London.
Phillipson, I. (1995), *How to Do Your Own PR*, How To Books, Plymouth.
White, J. (1994), *How to Understand and Manage Public Relations*, Random House, London.

9

Employing Outsiders

You will probably have to employ outside individuals and organizations at some stage in the proceedings in order to help you to run a winning conference. Clearly not all the key tasks and duties can be dealt with by you or be passed over automatically to the venue or overnight accommodation. You should therefore consider the pros and cons of commissioning outsiders, be able to identify the workload they will be taking on and feel confident that you can work well with them up to and beyond the event.

Commissioning outsiders

First, decide whether or not you should bring in outside assistance. Think about the types of individuals and organizations you might commission and the main benefits and drawbacks of using them before going on to make this decision.

Which outsiders are you most likely to commission to help you?

Those who can print and supply publicity material for your conference – pre-conference documents such as a 'What's On' guide, badges to be worn by participants, and conference documents such as a programme of activities? Are they therefore printers, tourist boards and convention bureaux?
  Others who can transport people and goods to and from the event

and between the venue and the overnight accommodation? In other words, taxi and minicab firms and possibly bus and coach operators?

Will you commission individuals and organizations to decorate the venue for you, put up banners and arrange flower displays – that is, printers again, designers and perhaps florists?

Those who will equip the conference for you by supplying equipment, facilities and services which are not available at the venue or overnight accommodation? Perhaps also audio-visual equipment hirers and employment agencies? Who else?

Others who will maintain security at the event, stop competitors from entering the conference rooms and equipment from leaving them? Security guards, then? Anyone else?

People and firms to provide catering – the reception, breaks, lunches, dinners, a banquet? Caterers, therefore?

Those who arrange social activities for partners during the business programme and for all participants? In that case they could be entertainers, tour operators – a potentially endless list!

Others who can provide insurance cover against cancellation or abandonment, physical damage to or by employees or the public, to or by your products? So, insurance companies?

What are the main benefits of using outside individuals and organizations?

Is it the specialist knowledge available? Will they have expertise in areas with which you are largely unfamiliar, such as printing publicity material, say? Are they capable of doing a job which you cannot do yourself? Or is greater experience the potential benefit? Do they have the hands-on experience that you do not possess, perhaps in transporting speakers, delegates and partners in the most pleasant and effective manner? Can they simply do a job better than you, avoiding the many mistakes you would probably make (especially first time around)?

Will using them give you more time? Can they carry out some of the more time-consuming tasks and duties for you, such as decorating the venue with signs and banners? Can they do a job as well as you and free your energies to be concentrated on other, more demanding work? Are they able to attend to various tasks and duties at a lower cost than would be incurred by you if these were completed in-house? Is it cheaper to bring in local administrative and secretarial assistance than to deploy your own staff from head office? They may be able to do a job as well as you but in a more cost-effective manner.

What are the drawbacks?

Lack of relevant knowledge about your particular situation may be one. Can they possibly know everything they need to know about your firm and the conference? It is not always easy to transfer such knowledge accurately and fully. Are they aware of the individual ways in which your company operates, including the procedures that need to be followed and the people who must be consulted? If they are not, what are the likely consequences?

Another drawback may be lack of commitment to the cause. Do they share your passion, your desire to succeed and your vision of a winning event? Is this just another job to them – one of many? Do they really care whether or not they contribute to a success or cause its failure? They may be interested only in obtaining payment, as much and as soon as possible. What are the potential results of this?

Incurring increased costs may also be a drawback. Are fees for specialists, catering and social activities excessive? They may be – although you have to set these against the financial savings, since outsiders may be able to negotiate better deals in their field than you can. As important, are you going to have to spend time providing the relevant knowledge that they need and chasing them to maintain commitment? Maybe – and time is money!

Will you use outside individuals and organizations? On what does your decision depend?

What you decide depends partly on the knowledge and expertise currently available to you in each particular area, both your own and that of colleagues and associates, at the venue and at the overnight accommodation. Is the expertise there to successfully produce publicity material, arrange transport, decorate the venue, equip the conference, provide security, see to catering arrangements and social activities, and to insure the event?

The time constraints imposed on you are also a factor. Do you have the time to carry out each and every task and duty yourself – to collect a speaker and his or her partner or tape a sign to a wall in the foyer? Should you not concentrate on the key activities, delegating others elsewhere? Can you leave them to do their work with occasional, rather than excessive and time-consuming, checks?

Take into account financial limitations, too. How far does your budget stretch, and how much have you set aside for specialist help and the necessary fees? Do you have the money to call in expert assistance?

Then again, allowing for the cost of your time, can outside help be brought in at a lower level than would be incurred in-house?

Sharing the workload

If you feel it is necessary or worthwhile to commission outsiders you should then move on to decide who does what, dividing up the various tasks and duties which need to be carried out.

Can they print or provide publicity material for you?

Such material includes pre-conference documents for speakers, delegates and their partners to be sent out regularly before the event to advise, inform and maintain interest. This may incorporate a revised programme of business and social activities – again stressing the benefits of attending – a 'What's On' guide for the area, a map with the venue, overnight accommodation, car parking facilities and places of interest highlighted on it, details of and paperwork for travel and accommodation. Remember to order spares in case some of the originals go astray or are mislaid.

It may also include badges to be handed out and worn by everyone at the conference for identification and security purposes. Decide which type – those that clip on to lapels or pockets rather than with sticky backs or safety pins? (Too much damage with them!) Should they be in your firm's colours, with its logo, too? Make sure that participants' names are printed clearly and correctly to avoid causing offence. (Don't let them write their own names – their handwriting may be illegible!) Should they have plastic covers, to increase durability?

Other publicity material includes conference documents for participants and their partners, such as a finalized programme of activities or up-to-date information – sales facts and figures or new product specifications perhaps. These are best given out with badges on arrival, rather than posted beforehand. Packaging and postage costs mount up, and documents may then be left behind. Again, order a sufficient number of spares.

How about transporting participants and products to and from the venue?

You may decide to use taxis or minicabs to transport speakers and their partners, either individually, or in couples. Should they be picked up from home or work, taken to and from the venue in style? Will, say, thirty or a hundred delegates and their partners be transported *en masse*? Do you need to lay on coaches and set pick-up points and drop-off points on return? During the conference, are taxis, minibuses and coaches needed to take them to and from the venue and overnight accommodation and out and about, if appropriate?

Will you transport products, a podium, a stage set, display units or stands, flip-charts, overhead projectors, televisions and camcorders by car, taxi or minicab? Will they be safe, and insured? Will you use a lorry, perhaps, for larger and more cumbersome items such as chairs, desks and tables for the conference rooms? Again, will they arrive undamaged – and insured, too, just in case?

Can outsiders decorate the venue on your behalf?

Can they put up signs, banners and sashes and set out flower arrangements? Will these be in the company's colours, perhaps emblazoned with the firm's logo, the theme of the conference or its main message? Are they all of good quality and clean and tidy from the start to the finish of the event? Have spares available, ready to replace damaged or tatty items as and when required.

What will the venue permit you to do, and where? Can you put signs in the car park so that participants and other users know exactly where to park? Are banners, sashes and flower arrangements acceptable in the foyer or at the entrances to the conference rooms you are occupying? Can you decorate the conference room itself? Ensure that any decoration conveys a professional image. Should it enliven the conference, perhaps? Does it properly convey your message?

Can they equip the conference for you, providing equipment, facilities and services which you need?

They may supply what the venue cannot – lapel microphones, perhaps, tripods, blackout curtains or even extension leads. At the overnight accommodation they could provide personal safes, a hairdresser and a beautician too. What else might be needed in your particular circumstances? They may replace other facilities that are available but are not up to standard, too old-fashioned, unreliable or just not good enough. At the venue, they might supply a film projector, camcorders and chairs. At the overnight accommodation, a photocopier and/or fax machine, maybe?

Can they supply security services?

Is this an issue? It may be! Are competitors likely to want to infiltrate your event to find out about your past performance or future plans? Are irreplaceable prototypes on display at that promotional conference to launch a new product? Is expensive equipment being used – projectors, camcorders, video players? Yes? Then you do need security!

You may therefore need strict registration procedures such as a registration desk by the entrance, staffed by two or more assistants. Names should be checked, badges handed out and worn at all times. Make polite but firm checks on unidentified people milling around and possibly regularly monitor comings and goings, particularly regarding equipment being moved about. You may need people there to make these checks – which should be done as politely as possible.

What about catering arrangements?

Figures 9.1, 9.2 and 9.3 on pages 135, 136 and 137–139 give examples of lunch, dinner and banquet menus.

A reception To open the conference for you and to allow the participants to meet each other, mingle and relax? Should you have soft rather than alcoholic drinks and a good range of finger snacks for all tastes including diabetics, vegetarians, those on diets and special diets for health reasons? Should it be held at the venue, at the overnight accommodation or somewhere more important, perhaps?

Breaks Throughout the programme? To provide breathing space and a chance to unwind? Should you provide tea, coffee, orange juice, apple juice, soft drinks (but not fizzy ones) biscuits, Danish pastries, possibly, and anything else which is light and easy to digest?

Lunches To begin the event? At midday, typically? At the venue or elsewhere? Will participants want to socialize or discuss issues covered to date? Should you provide non-alcoholic drinks – so participants remain bright and alert – a finger buffet with vol-au-vents, quiches, sausages and cheeses to cater for all palates? Bite-sized, easy-to-handle food which is simple to collect without having to queue? Or will you provide prompt and efficient service?

Dinners Half-way through the event, maybe, or in the early evening before a social activity starts? To socialize again and talk over the day's

BUFFETS

FISH BUFFET

Calmari Fries & Marie Rose Dip
Deep Fried King Prawns with Spicy Dip
Goujons of Plaice
Cockles & Mussels
Deorated Salmon
with Hollandaise Sauce
Dressed Cromer Crab
Smoked Oyster & Savoury Rice
Hot Jacket Potatoes
Served with a Selection of Five Salads
Fruit Salad
Profiteroles with Chocolate Sauce
Fresh Coffee and Cream

HOT FORK BUFFET

Spicy Chicken Wings
Chilli Con Carne
Chicken A La King
Stir Fried Vegetables
Spicy Meatballs
Saffron Rice
Jacket Potatoes
Five Assorted Salads
Black Forest Gateaux & Fresh cream
Sherry Trifle
Fresh Coffee and Cream

FINGER BUFFET

MENU A

Ham, Egg & Mushroom Vol-au-Vants
Cocktail Sausages Rolls
Assorted Sandwiches
Various Quiches
Cocktail Sausages with Dips
Crisps & Nuts
Assorted Bridge Rolls
Fresh Coffee and Cream

MENU B

Spiced Chicken Drumsticks
Cocktail Sausages with Dips
Ham, Egg & Mushgroom Vol-au-Vents
Cheese & Pineapple
Assorted Bridge Rolls
Cocktail Sausage Rolls
Assorted Sandwiches

Fresh Coffee and Cream

'CELEBRATION BUFFET'

Whole King Prawns with Garlic Mayonnaise
Roast Sirloin of Beef with Tomato and Horseradish Baskets
Chicken Drumsticks
Deep Fried Strips of Lemon Sole with Tartate Sauce Dips

Hot New Potatoes

Mexican Salad

Salad Nicoise

Apple and Celery Salad

Rice Salad

Wholemeal Rolls and Butter
Fresh Coffee
and Cream
Mints

3

BUFFETS

BUFFET A

Honey Roast Ham

Roast Norfolk Turkey

Cocktail Sausages & Dips

Hot Jacket Potatoe

Choice of Quiches

Granary Rolls & Butter

Four Assorted Salads

Savoury Rice

Black Forest Gateaux

and Fresh Cream

Fresh Coffee and Cream

BUFFET B

Honey Roast Ham

Cocktail Sausage Rolls

Chicken Drumsticks

Hot Jacket Potatoes

Assorted Vol-au-Vents

Granary Rolls & Butter

Four Assorted Salads

Savour Rice

Sherry Trifle

Fresh Coffee and Cream

BUFFET C

HOT PORK BUFFET

Chilli Con Carne

Chicken A La King

Saffron Rice

Stir Fry Vegetables

Spicy Meat Balls

Jacket Potatoes

Four Assorted Salads

Granary Rolls & Butter

Sherry Trifle

Fresh Coffee and Cream

4

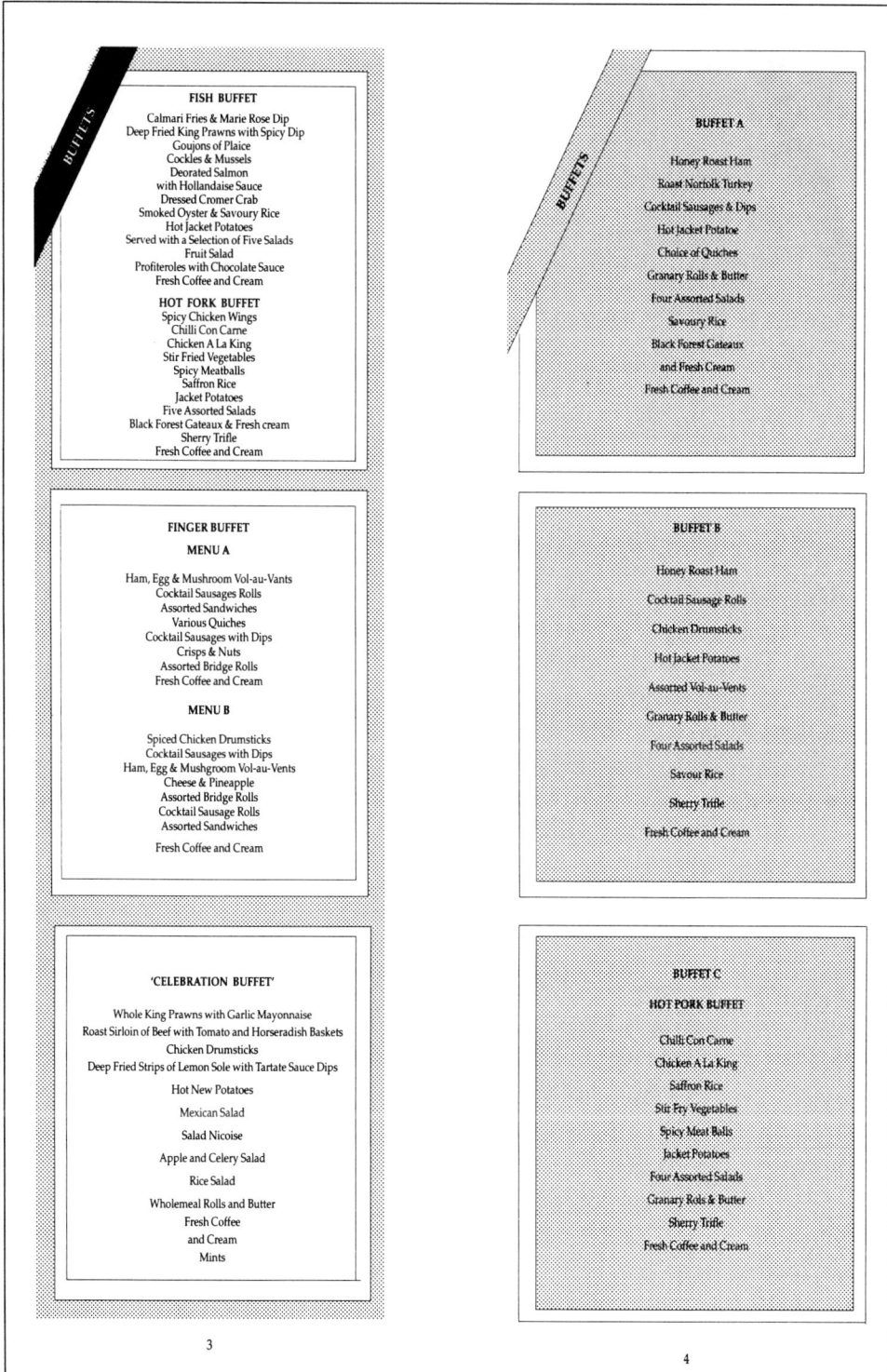

Figure 9.1   Lunch menus

MENUS

MENU A

Italian Minestrone Soup
-
Seafood Cocktail
-
Supreme of Chicken with a Cream Sauce
of Wine & Mushrooms
-
Seasonal Vegetables
-
Black Forest Gateaux
Flavoured with Kirsch
-
A selection of English Cheeses
-
Coffee with After Eight Mints
-
3 or 4 Course Available

MENU B

Marina Tropical Cocktail
Melon Balls, Kiwi Fruit and Mandarin
with Classic Liquer
-
Pached Salmon in a Prawn Marie Rose Sauce
-
Fillet of Beef Wellington
Baked in a Pastry Case with Maderia Pate
-
Selection of Seasonal Vegetables
-
Chocolate Mousse
with
Whipped Cream
-
Coffee
with
After Eight Mints
-
3 or 4 Course Available

MENU C

Terrine of Pate Maison
with Cumberland Sauce
-
Cream of Asparagus Soup
-
Half of Roast Spring Chicken
with Sausage & Herb Stuffing
served with Traditional Bread Sauce
-
Selection of Seasonal Vegetables
-
Fresh Fruit Salad flavoured with Kirsch
& Fresh Cream
-
Selection of English Cheeses
-
Coffee
with
After Eight Mints
-
3 or 4 Course Available

1

MENUS

MENU D

Marina Tropical Cocktail
Melon Balls, Kiwi Fruit, Mandarin
with Casis Liquer
-
French Onion Soup
-
Traditional Roast Sirloin of Beef
with Yorkshire Pudding
Roast Potatoes and Seasonal Vegetables
-
Dutch Apple Tart
with
Fresh Cream
-
Selection of English Cheeses
-
Coffee
with
After Eight Mints
-
3 or 4 Course Available

MENU E

Cream of Mushroom Soup
-
Poached Salmon & Pears with
Hollandaise Sauce
-
Traditional Roast Norfolk Turkey
with Chipolata, Bacon Rolls & Stuffing
served with Cranberry Sauce
-
Seasonal Vegetables
-
Cherry Pie and Fresh Cream
-
A selection of English Cheeses
-
Coffee with After Eight Mints
-
3 or 4 Course Available

MENU F

Advocado Prawns
in a Marie Rose Sauce
-
Spring Vegetable Soup
-
Sirloin Steak Chasseur with
Selection of Seasonal Vegetables
-
Profiteroles with Chocolate Sauce
-
A Selection of English Cheeses
-
Coffee with
After Eight Mints
-
3 or 4 Course Available

2

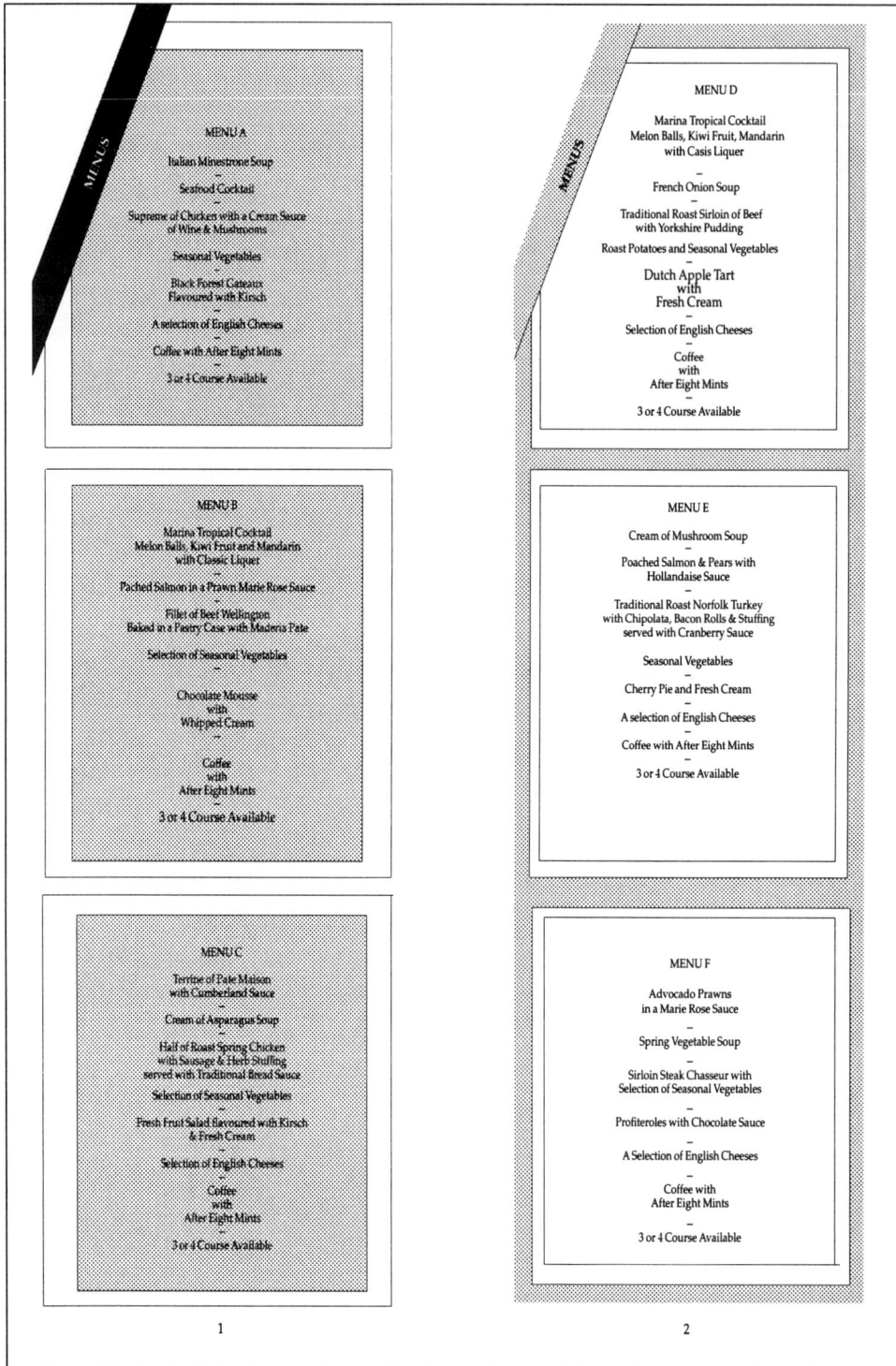

Figure 9.2   Dinner menus

Banqueting Menu Selector and Wine List

Soup

Cream of Tomato and Orange
£2.45

Cream of Vegetable
£2.45

Cream of Chicken with Toasted Almonds
£2.50

Cream of Celery and Watercress
£2.50

Lentil Soup with Sippets
£2.45

Gazpacho
(*chilled Spanish Soup*)
£2.65

Broccoli with Stilton
£2.85

Brown Windsor
(*Beef Soup enfused with Red Wine*)
£2.85

Cream of Mushroom
£2.65

Seafood Bisque
£3.75

Fish

	Intermediate Course	Main Course
Poached Supreme of Salmon Hollandaise	£5.95	£11.75
Braised Halibut Steak with Prawn and Lobster Sauce	£6.95	£12.97
Fillet of Sole Bonne Femme	£5.25	£9.75
Brochette of Scallop and Monkfish with Saffron Sauce	£5.95	£11.75
Grilled Fillets of Lemon Sole with Lemon and Lime Butter	£5.50	£10.25
Grilled Rainbow Trout served with a mellow Almond Butter	£4.95	£9.25
Cabbage Parcels with a filling of Crab and Prawns served with a Hot Tomato Coulis		
Poached Fillets of Plaice with a White Wine Sauce garnished with Mussels	£5.15	£10.50
Poached Medallions of Monkfish with a Coarse Grain Mustard Sauce	£4.25	£8.75
	£5.35	£10.70

Main Courses

All main courses are served with Bouquetiere of Fresh Vegetables and Potatoes

Venison

Roast Haunch of Venison with a rich Madeira Sauce
£9.75

Casserole of Venison with Redcurrant & Port Sauce
£9.50

Chicken

Half Spring Chicken served with Roast Gravy, Sage and Onion Stuffing and Bacon Roll
£9.75

Breast of Chicken stuffed with Asparagus served with a Cream and White Wine Sauce
£9.85

Roast Chicken with a Hunter Sauce of Red Wine, Baby Onions, Mushrooms and Tarragon
£9.55

Poached Breast of Chicken served with a Creamy Sherry Sauce garnished with Julienne of Red and Green Peppers
£9.85

Pan fried Breast of Chicken stuffed with Apricots served with a cream sauce warmed with Brandy
£9.95

THE AUBREY PARK HOTEL

All prices inclusive of VAT @ 17.5%

Figure 9.3 Banquet meals

Banqueting Menu Selector and Wine List

Lamb

Grilled Lamb Cutlets with a Port Sauce
£8.85

Roast Leg of Lamb with Mint Sauce
£8.60

Casserole of Lamb Dijonnaise served with Rice
£8.85

Brochettes of Lamb served with Rice, Tomato and Basil Sauce
£8.85

Saddle of Lamb stuffed with a Sage and Onion Stuffing
£8.40

Beef

Roast Sirloin of Beef with a Rich Red Wine and Mushroom Sauce
£10.45

Sauté of Beef Stroganoff served with Braised Rice
£10.35

8oz Sirloin Steak served with a Port Wine Sauce
£10.45

Roast Rib of Beef served with Yorkshire Pudding and Horseradish
£10.05

Sauté Beef Bourgvignone with Rice
£10.25

Fillet of Beef Wellington
£13.35

Duck

Duck Breast Pan fried and served with a Blackcurrant Sauce
£10.35

Duck Breast Oven baked and served with a clear Strawberry and Black Peppercorn Sauce
£10.35

PORK

Roast Loin of Pork stuffed with a Sweet Fruit Stuffing
£8.75

Medallion of Pork with Dijon Mustard Sauce
£9.95

Grilled Pork Cutlet with an Apple and Brandy Sauce
£8.75

Roast Leg of Pork with a Seville Sauce
£8.55

Casseroled Pork Sweet and Sour served with Rice
£8.45

All prices inclusive of VAT @ 17.5%

As an alternative to the bouquetiere of vegetables and potatoes, below are a few suggested variations, these carry a 90p surcharge for each one chosen.

Selection of Vegetables

Ratatouille	Braised Celery
Baton Carrots	Sweetcorn Niblets
Vichy Carrots	& Peppers
Broccoli Spears	Baby Sweetcorn
and Almonds	Runner Beans
Braised Onions	Red Cabbage
Cauliflower Frits	Spinach & Cream
Cauliflower Cheese	Stir-Fry Vegetables
Mange Tout	Courgettes Provencal
Brussel Sprouts	
Caramelised Parsnips	

Our Chef will be only too pleased to quote prices for seasonal vegetables.

Selection of Potatoes

Sàute	Parisienne
Baked Jacket Potatoes	Roast
Lyonnaise	New Potatoes Minted
Fondant	Fried Potatoes
Boulangere	Parmentier
Duchess	Delmonico
Marquis	Croquette

Selection of Salads
£2.25

Green Salad
Mixed Salad
Tomato & Onion Salad
Seasonal Leaves & Avocado

Figure 9.3   Banquet meals (continued)

138

Banqueting Menu Selector and Wine List

CONFERENCE AND BANQUETING MENU SELECTORS

The following dishes are listed and priced separately in order that you may select the ideal menu for your event. The Chef and his team however, will be happy to assist and even offer written suggestions of sample menus.

All prices inclusive of VAT @ 17.5%

Starters

Melon and Grapefruit Cocktail marinated in Creme de Menthe
£2.50

A Crown of Ogen Melon filled with Fresh Pineapple and a Creamy Coconut Sorbet
£4.50

Fan of Avocado served with Plump Prawns in a Marie Rose Sauce
£3.95

Egg Harlequin
(*Boiled Egg coated half with a Marie Rose Sauce — half with Mayonnaise accompanied with a Salad garnish*)
£2.90

Chef's Game Pâte served with Cumberland Sauce and Melba Toast
£3.95

Hot Seafood Vol au Vents
(*Choice Seafood accompanied with a White Wine Sauce laid in three Puff Pastry Vol au Vents*)
£3.25

Sauted Button Mushrooms served with a Tomato and Basil Sauce
£3.25

Salad of Hot Chicken Livers with a Raspberry Vinaigrette
£2.75

Salmon Mousse served with a Lemon and Dill Mayonnaise
£3.95

Slices of Sweet Melon served with Ribbons of Palma Ham
£3.75

Smoked Chicken and Avocado Pear served with Seasonal Leaves
£3.25

Brie and Mushrooms Fritters served with a Cranberry and Ginger Chutney
£3.50

Stir Fried Chicken and Cashew Nuts in an Oyster and Hoi Sin Sauce accompanied with Noodles
£3.75

Tropical Fruit Cocktail lightly flavoured with Dark Rum
£3.15

Smoked Fillet of Trout served with Lemon and Cucumber Dressing
£4.25

Smoked Salmon, Seasonal Leaves and Lemon
£7.95

THE AUBREY PARK HOTEL

Figure 9.3 Banquet meals (concluded)

programme? Should you supply a limited range of alcoholic drinks (at last!)? Should there be plated meals of three or four easily digestible courses, making due allowances for special diets? Service should be swift and discreet throughout. Should the dinner be at the venue, at the overnight accommodation or at a restaurant, possibly?

A banquet   To close the event? Held in the evening (into the early hours!)? A last chance to socialize, strike deals and put across your message, and a final opportunity to eat, drink and be merry? There should be alcohol available and good food suited to the participants' tastes. Should the banquet be held at the venue, at the overnight accommodation or somewhere extra special – the best restaurant, or a medieval hall perhaps?

Can they manage social activities for you too?

Refer to Figure 9.4 on pages 141–150 for examples of social activities.

What about partners' activities while speakers and delegates are occupied during the business programme? Can outsiders bring entertainments, such as carpet bowls or quizzes, into the venue or overnight accommodation? Can they take partners out for the morning, afternoon or day on a sightseeing tour, visit to an art gallery, museum or whatever?

Outsiders may also manage speakers', delegates' and partners' activities after business hours – a treasure hunt or music and dancing perhaps. Will they provide these at the venue or overnight accommodation? Can they offer outside activities such as ten-pin bowling, pony trekking and steam train rides? (The activities must *all* be optional *and* suited to everyone's tastes.)

Will you need to take out any additional insurance cover above and beyond what is held already by your firm? At the conference venue? At the overnight accommodation?

Figure 9.5 on pages 152–155 is an example of an insurance plan you might need.

Cancellation or abandonment   In case the event has to be cancelled or curtailed for reasons beyond your control, such as terrorist activity or an oubreak of infectious disease? In case of cancellation by speakers, necessitating replacing them with others at extra cost, or delegates

---

Social Activities

Merseyside Tourism & Conference Bureau can organise tailor-made social and spouse programmes for conferences taking place in the area. We have a team of MerseyGuides who are all blue badge trained and they are available for a variety of tours and excursions.

The following are examples of the types of half day and full day tours we can offer.

1.   Liverpool City Sightseeing Tour

(One and a half hour tour)

A guided coach tour taking in the "Highlights of Liverpool".
See the Victorian and Georgian splendour of what was once the second city of the British Empire.

The tour also includes the famous Pier Head, Albert Dock, tales of eminent people and the history of the port.

An optional extra would be a refreshment stop at Liverpool Cathedral.

2.   Wirral Tour

(Half day tour)

Travel by coach to the picturesque village of Port Sunlight on the Wirral Peninsula. Enjoy a guided tour of this model industrial village built in the late 19th century by Viscount Leverhulme to house the workers of his soap factory.

Visit the Lady Lever Art Gallery, one of the most beautiful art museums in the world.

After refreshments at the gallery return to Liverpool crossing the River Mersey on a famous Mersey Ferry.

Figure 9.4   Social activities

3. Liverpool Heritage Walk

(Two hour tour)

A guided walking tour round the centre of one of Britain's most fascinating cities.

Refreshments can be included.

4. Beatles Magical History Tour

(Two hour tour)

The Beatles are Liverpool's famous sons. This tour will fascinate you - even if you are not a fan of the Fab Four.

Tour of Beatle sights and sounds including Penny Lane, Strawberry Field, Cavern Walks and Mathew Street.

Optional visit to The Beatles Story, the museum that recreates the sights and the sounds of the sixties.

5. Speke Hall

(Half day tour)

A guided tour of Speke Hall. Rich half-timbering characterises this lovely Elizabethan Manor House.

Communal living in Tudor times is recalled in the Great Hall and priest holes remind us of the dangers experienced by Catholic priests in 16th Century England.

After coffee an opportunity to explore the garden and woodland

Figure 9.4   Social activities (continued)

6. Ness Gardens

(Half day tour)

Ness Gardens, the botanic gardens of Liverpool University, cover 62 acres of the Wirral, overlooking the River Dee and the Welsh Hills.

They are said to be the most outstanding learning gardens in Britain, with beauty and interest for every season.

7. Pilkington Glass Museum

(Half day tour)

A chance to visit the Pilkington Glass Museum at St Helens, where you will be given a conducted tour to explore the history and manufacture of glass. Take a look at 4,000 years of glass-making.

The museum has an outstanding antique glass collection, ranging from a rare ancient Egyptian amphoriskos to the very latest modern glass sculptures.

Two full size working exhibits are the Clare Island Lighthouse Optic and a working periscope giving views across the lake. There are many other inter-active exhibits.

8. Ellesmere Port Boat Museum

(Half day tour)

The coach will drive from Liverpool to the base of the Wirral Peninsula to Ellesmere Port. Here the Boat Museum houses the largest floating collection of canal craft in the world.

The museum is housed in the restored buildings of the old dock complex, dating back to the 19th Century.

Figure 9.4   Social activities (continued)

9. Albert Dock

*(Walking tour approximately one hour
or half day including visits to attractions)*

*A walking tour of the Albert Dock, which is a symbol of the revival of Liverpool
and as the most ambitious waterfront regeneration scheme in Europe, has
become the blueprint for such schemes both in the UK and abroad.*

*Today the warehouses are, once again, an Aladdin's cave of goods from all over
the world - Indian Silks, Austrian glass, French perfume and lots more.*

*The tour can include a visit to the Merseyside Maritime Museum, providing a
fascinating insight into Liverpool's nautical heritage and a visit to the Tate
Gallery. The Tate opened in May 1988 has already established itself as the
National collection of Modern Art in the North of England, and as a major
international force.*

Refreshments can be taken in an Albert Dock cafe or the Maritime Museum.

10. Prescot Museum of Clock and Watchmaking

(Half day tour)

*Prescot was the main centre of the South Lancashire watch trade in the 18th and
19th centuries and its products were famous at home and abroad*

*The Museum's exhibitions illustrate the craft of clock, watch and toolmaking and
the social background to these trades.*

There is a reconstruction of a traditional Lancashire Watchmaker's workshop.

Figure 9.4 Social activities (continued)

11. Martin Mere

(Half day tour)

Martin Mere is a 350-acre wildfowl and wetlands centre where you can see rare and exotic birds from all over the world.

12. Manchester Museum of Science and Industry and Granada Studios Tour

(Full day tour)

In the morning visit the Museum of Science and Industry on the site of the worlds oldest passenger railway station. Marvel at planes that made flying history in the Air Space Gallery, see the story of steam power, show how electricity has changed our lives.

Lunch in the cafe before a short walk to Granada Studios.

In the afternoon Granada Studios - a two hour guided tour behind the scenes of television. Visit the famous Coronation Street, Downing Street, the House of Commons and journey down Baker Street.

Figure 9.4 Social activities (continued)

---

13. Chester and Chirk Castle

(Full day tour)

A guided coach tour of the historic city of Chester. Famed for its picturesque streets and unique medieval rows, it has the only complete circuit of city walls in England and evidence of nearly every period of history since Roman times.

Lunch will be available at an Hotel in Chester.

Then on to Chirk Castle, a Marches fortress with fine views, elegant state rooms with elaborate plasterwork, superb Adam-style furniture, tapestries and portraits. Formal gardens and 18th century parkland.

Afternoon tea can be served in the Castle's tea rooms.

---

14. York

(Full day tour)

Coach trip to the majestic city of York. After coffee enjoy a guided walking tour taking in the rich history of this walled city.

After lunch a journey into the days when the Vikings settled in York. See how they lived and worked in the award winning Jorvik Centre.

Then free time for you to discover York for yourself - the Minster, Castle Museum or browsing in the shops along the medieval 'Shambles'.

Figure 9.4   Social activities (continued)

---

15. Lancaster

(Full day tour)

The city of Lancaster has an abundance of history dating back to Roman times.

Many of the buildings of interest can be visited during the guided walk around the city.

Visits can be arranged to the Medieval Castle, with its magnificent views over the city and its surrounding countryside, the Aston Memorial with its Edwardian elegance and the Judge's lodgings with its two fine museums.

Refreshments can be organised.

Figure 9.4 Social activities (continued)

MerseyGuide Services

Merseyside's team of Blue Badge trained guides can offer a wide range of services:

Tours and Social Programmes

Large and small groups can be catered for from a 12 seater minibus to a 60 seater coach. All tastes can be catered for from Liverpool's fine architecture to the Beatles.

Talks

With their tremendous local knowledge, Merseyguides are available to give presentations to social groups, clubs and societies on such themes as Merseyside's social history, fine arts and famous people.

Assisting with Business Clients and VIP Visitors

Guides can assist in planning an itinerary for business clients and their partners. This could include a private guided tour for the spouse of a major client or an internal VIP visitor such as the Chairman.

Merseyside Tourism & Conference Bureau's professional tourist guides can provide chauffeur-driven tours, a 'meet and greet' facility and foreign language speakers. This service relieves organisations of the problematic aspects of such visits and ensures that clients receive the best possible welcome on Merseyside.

Selling Merseyside to New Recruits

Recruitment of external senior employees for positions in Merseyside often presents a difficulty caused by lack of accurate knowledge on the high quality of life offered by the area. We are able to provide tours for individual candidates and their families or for groups. Particular emphasis is given to desirable residential areas, schools, shopping, cultural and sporting opportunities.

Figure 9.4   Social activities (continued)

Evening Events

THEATRE EVENING

At the Liverpool Playhouse, the oldest repertory theatre in the country.

The theatre has a varied and lively programme throughout the year and has played host to such famous productions as 'Shirley Valentine', 'Educating Rita' and 'Stags and Hens'.

The evening could include drinks before the performance and during the interval in the Executive Lounge and supper afterwards in a nearby city centre hotel.

BEATLES EVENING

Re-live the sights and sounds of the sixties at Beatles Story in the Albert Dock.

Begin the evening with a welcome drink and private tour of the exhibition tracing their careers from the early days up to the present time.

Then into the authentic reconstruction of the Cavern Club complete with live 60s band or 60s disco.

Bar facilities and a full range of buffet menus are also available.

Alternatively you can soak in the atmosphere and dance the night away in the Cavern Club on Mathew Street.

Figure 9.4 Social activities (continued)

MERSEYSIDE MARITIME MUSEUM

The Maritime Museum, in the historic Albert Dock complex, offers a wide range of evening entertainment.

An evening reception and private viewing of the 'Emigrants to the New World' exhibition, which vividly portrays the nineteenth century exodus of people leaving Liverpool for the New World. Delegates can be served grog and plain ships biscuits in the Foyer, make their way through the exhibition and chat to "Emigrants" en route for America. Then on reaching the other side are greeted with canapes and Manhattan cocktails.

Or invite your delegates to a Maritime Evening in the 2nd or 3rd floor galleries including private viewing of the exhibition, a sea shanty band and hot pot supper.

For a formal occasion or conference dinner, the museum can open its 4th floor restaurant for a silver service dinner for up to 200 delegates.

CHINESE BANQUET

Liverpool has the oldest Chinese Community in Europe and a range of excellent Chinese Restaurants.

A number of restaurants are large enough to cater for a private party of 100 delegates for a sumptuous Chinese Banquet.

MERSEY FERRY CRUISE

See the Liverpool waterfront by night from a famous Mersey Ferry.

The cruise can include a commentary on the history of Liverpool and Birkenhead, buffet and bar facilities.

Figure 9.4 Social activities (concluded)

deciding not to attend? Enforced reduced attendance? Outside influences, such as train strikes, air delays or bad weather, limiting the numbers attending to non-profitable levels? Failure to vacate? Unable to remove participants and products on time?

Physical damage Employers' liability in case of bodily injury sustained by your employees? Public liability to cover you against your responsibility to third parties for causing personal injury, death or damage to property? Product liability in case your products harm other people or property? Make absolutely sure you are well covered at the venue *and* the overnight accommodation.

Travel insurance and personal accident benefits To cover temporary, total and partial disablement and even death? Emergency travel expenses in case alternative and costly transport arrangements need to be made at short notice?

Personal money and effects To cover lost or stolen cash and belongings and misuse of credit cards? For you *and* your colleagues? Speakers *and* partners? Delegates *and* partners?

Money and door registration receipts To cover cash, banknotes, cheques, credit card slips and so on stolen or lost at the venue? Also in transit from the venue directly en route to a bank in the locality of the conference?

Working with outsiders

It is then wise to consider how you should negotiate and work with outside individuals and organizations so that their work rate and performance are as good as they can be and you are satisfied with the results.

What qualities in particular should you look for in outsiders?

Trustworthy and a good reputation With an ethical approach to business – offering impartial advice, maintaining confidentiality and disclosing any conflicting interests to you, perhaps? Check that they are financially stable to minimize the risk that they will cease trading before or during the work they are doing for you – especially important if you are providing an upfront payment! Proof of stability may be provided

insurex
EXPO-SURE
GROUP

EXHIBITION CONFERENCE AND EVENT INSURANCE PLAN

Brief Summary of coverage
(If full details are required we will send a specimen policy wording if requested)

PART 1 **CANCELLATION OR ABANDONMENT**
Coverage option insured: Superior Plus or Superior or Essential
Limit of Indemnity: As shown on Proposal Form

		Superior Plus	or	Superior	or	Essential
A1	Cancellation Abandonment etc.	Yes		Yes		Yes
A2	Non-appearance of speakers or entertainers	Yes		Yes		Yes
A3	Failure to Vacate Facility	Yes		Yes		Yes
A4	Enforced Reduced Attendance	Yes		No		No

Losses covered for selected coverage option shown above.

BASIS OF INDEMNITY FOR SELECTED COVERAGE OPTION SHOWN:
limit each item i.e. maximum recoverable as % of limit of indemnity

		Superior Plus	or	Superior	or	Essential
B1	Expenses of organisation	100%		100%		100%
B2	Cost of advising exhibitors/delegates etc.	100%		100%		100%
B3	Return of fees for attendance, space & advertising	100%		100%		25%
B4	Penalties for Failure to vacate	40%		20%		10%
B5	Net Income (i.e. profit)	100%		100%		NIL
B6	Contingent Responsibilities	40%		20%		10%
B7	Remedial Action costs i.e.					
	Cost unauthorised by U/writers	100%		20%		10%
	Cost authorised by U/writers	100%		100%		100%
B8	Protective action costs for next Event	20%		NIL		NIL

PRINCIPAL EXCLUSIONS:— 1. Financial Causes 2. Lack of support 3. Pre-existing loss 4. War and related risks*
6. Terrorism outside country of Event*
* Cover can be extended on payment of additional premium.

PART 2 **PHYSICAL DAMAGE TO PROPERTY**

A1. "All Risks" on property of Insured for which they are responsible excluding items more specifically insured by Part A2 below.

Limit of Indemnity
£25,000 any one "Event"

A2. The following property provided to the Insured by the property owners or management of the "Venue" for the purpose of the Insured "Event": Buildings and machinery, plant, fixtures and fittings.

£10,000 any one loss

FURTHER INFORMATION FROM:
INSUREX/EXPO-SURE GROUP,
THE PANTILES HOUSE,
2 NEVILL STREET,
ROYAL TUNBRIDGE WELLS,
KENT TN2 5SA.
TEL: 0892 511500 FAX: 0892 510016

the
MEETINGS
INDUSTRY
a s s o c i a t i o n

Figure 9.5 Insurance plan

PART 3   **LEGAL LIABILITIES**

1.   CONTINGENT EMPLOYERS' LIABILITY   **Limit of Liability**

    NOTE:— Employers, Liability Certificates to comply with laws relating to compulsory insurance of liability to employees in Great Britain, Northern Ireland, the Isle of Man or the Channel Islands are available on application.   Unlimited

2.   CONTINGENT PUBLIC LIABILITY
    Includes legal liability for Contractual liability loss or damage to buildings and their contents temporarily occupied for the purposes of the "Event" and Contractual Liability.   £1,000,000 any one occurrence

3.   PRODUCTS LIABILITY   £1,000,000 in the aggregate any one "Event"

4.   DEDUCTIBLE
    £50 each and every loss for "Events" held in the United Kingdom or £100 each and every loss for "Events" held elsewhere.

PART 4   **TRAVEL INSURANCE** (OPTIONAL EXTENSION ONLY)

A.   Personal Accident Benefits (per "Insured Person")

	SINGLE BENEFITS	DOUBLE BENEFITS
(i) Death	£5,000 **	£10,000 **
(ii) Loss of sight, hands or feet or loss of use	£5,000	£10,000
(iii) Permanent total disablement	£5,000	£10,000
(iv) Temporary total disablement	£50 per week*	£100 per week *
(v) Temporary partial disablement	£20 per week*	£40 per week *

*   Maximum period of benefit 104 weeks from date of first disablement
*   The weekly benefits A (iv) and (v) above shall not apply in respect of any 'Insured Person' who is not normally gainfully employed
** Limited to £1,000 for persons under 16 or over 70 years of age.

Compensation shall not be payable for any one 'Insured Person' under more than one of the Benefits A (i), (ii), (iii) for the same accident. The amount of any weekly compensation paid shall be deducted from compensation subsequently becoming payable under Benefits A (i), (ii) or (iii).

	SINGLE BENEFITS	DOUBLE BENEFITS	DEDUCTIBLE
B Medical and Emergency Travel Expenses	£5,000 in all any one "Event"	£10,000 in all any one "Event"	£25 any one loss
C (i) Personal Effects	£750	£1,000	£50 for "Events" in the United Kingdom or £100 for "Events" held elsewhere
(ii) Personal Money	£200	£250	
(iii) Misuse of Credit Cards	£250	£350	
D Cancellation/Curtailment	£750 in all any one "Event"	£1,250 in all any one "Event"	
E Personal Liability	£500,000 any one occurrence	£1,000,000 any one occurrence	

IMPORTANT
You can increase the single or double benefits to even higher limits if you so wish. Contact Insurex Expo-Sure Group Ltd. for details.

This covers the persons officially known by you to be travelling and who will be included in the declaration of total numbers to be made. No cover applies to wives, children or friends of the 'insured persons' unless officially recorded by you as an 'insured person'.

PART 5   **MONEY AND DOOR REGISTRATION RECEIPTS** (OPTIONAL EXTENSION ONLY)

    LIMIT OF INDEMNITY

1.   Money at the "Venue" and in transit from "Venue" directly en route to a bank in the vicinity of the "Event"   £5,000 any one loss

2.   Money being on the day door receipts paid in cash, banknotes, cheques and other negotiable instruments at the "Venue" for door registration and tickets directly associated with the "Event" or whilst contained in a locked safe.   DEDUCTIBLE

    £50 any one loss

Figure 9.5   Insurance plan (continued)

insurex
EXPO-SURE
GROUP

THE PANTILES HOUSE, 2 NEVILL STREET,
ROYAL TUNBRIDGE WELLS, KENT TN2 5SA.
TEL: 0892 511500 FAX: 0892 510016

Exhibition, Conference and Event Insurance Specialists

EXHIBITION, CONFERENCE & EVENT INSURANCE PROPOSAL

Deletion of exclusions and conditions can be requested by the applicant but no alteration to the standard cover is effective until the insurers have accepted the alteration and detailed any additional conditions and premiums by endorsement.
Where more than one Event is to be insured list these separately and if any answers to the questions are not the same for each Event any exceptions should be listed.

1 — INSURED

Name _____

Address _____

_____

_____

_____ postcode _____

Telephone _____

Fax _____

2 — EVENT TO BE INSURED

Name of Event _____

Dates of tenancy (including build up and breakdown)

From _____ To _____

Open dates

From _____ To _____

3 — VENUE(S) WHERE THE PRINCIPAL ACTIVITIES OF EVENT TO BE HELD

Name _____

Address _____

_____

_____

_____ postcode _____

a) Is any part of Event to be held in the open, in a tent, marquee or in a temporary structure? If so is cover required for adverse weather?

☐ Yes ☐ No

b) Are there any known construction, alteration or repair works or planned at the Venue(s), prior to completion of your Event? If so is cover required?

☐ Yes ☐ No

(The policy excludes losses arising from above unless arranged with the insurers)

4 — TYPE OF EVENT

a) Conference/meeting/congress/exhibition (please delete as applicable)

☐ Without exhibits   ☐ with exhibits

☐ open to the public   ☐ not open to the public   ☐ with seminars or workshop speakers

b) Other type of Event

☐ ie. incentive travel, product launch, corporate hospitality etc.
Please give details.

c) Will the Event use teleconferencing? If so do you require cover?   ☐ Yes ☐ No

(The policy excludes loss arising from teleconferencing unless agreed by insurers.)

d) Is your Event dependent upon another Event? If so give details.   ☐ Yes ☐ No

5 — FINANCIAL INFORMATION

a) Please state currency if not Sterling.

BUDGETED GROSS REVENUE
FROM ALL SOURCES: £ _____

BUDGETED EXPENSES: £ _____

BUDGETED NET INCOME: £ _____

b) Does another party have an interest in the Gross Revenue?   ☐ Yes ☐ No

c) Does the Gross Revenue represent the total revenue from the Event?   ☐ Yes ☐ No

d) Will there be any income from the sale of television or advertising rights?   ☐ Yes ☐ No

e) Do you maintain records of current and past Events?   ☐ Yes ☐ No

f) Is any finance provided by sponsors?   ☐ Yes ☐ No

g) Does the fee for attendance include travel and accommodation costs of delegates or exhibitors?   ☐ Yes ☐ No

BDK/UK 9/92/4

© 1992 COPYRIGHT BPD KELLETT & CO. LTD.

Figure 9.5   Insurance plan (continued)

6 — EVENT SPEAKERS

a) Is the Event dependent on two or fewer key or celebrity speakers?   ☐ Yes ☐ No

b) Will there be entertainers or the like performing?   ☐ Yes ☐ No

c) If either of these covers is required, please give details for each speaker or entertainer of their:
   i) age;   iii) where travelling from;
   ii) health;   iv) how travelling;
   v) how long ahead of their presentation, performance or rehearsals they will be arriving in the city where the Event is held.

7 — CONTRACT WITH VENUE(S) AND PRELIMINARY ARRANGEMENTS

a) Do written contracts of hire exist between yourselves and the Venue(s)?   ☐ Yes ☐ No

b) Have you made adequate preliminary arrangements to ensure a satisfactory Event?   ☐ Yes ☐ No

If No, please give details.

8 — EVENT INFORMATION

a) Please state approximately how many of each of the following are anticipated.
   Exhibitors _____   Delegates _____

   Trade visitors _____   Paying visitors _____

b) Has this Event been held: on at least three previous occasions?   ☐ Yes ☐ No

c) If known, what approximate proportion of exhibitors and delegates are estimated to originate from:

	% exhibitors	% delegates
UK & Channel Islands	___	___
Europe & Scandinavia	___	___
North & South America	___	___
Africa & Asia	___	___
Australia & New Zealand	___	___

9 — PRE-EXISTING POTENTIAL LOSS

Are you aware of any matter, fact, circumstance or incidents existing or threatened, that could affect your Event and result in a claim under this insurance?   ☐ Yes ☐ No

If Yes, please give details.
NOTE: If you become aware of any such circumstances after completing this proposal, you must disclose the circumstances to the insurers immediately. Failure to advise could result in any claim arising from these circumstances being denied.

10 — LOSS EXPERIENCE

At any time within the last 5 years, has your organisation had a loss, or encountered circumstances or incidents, which could lead to a loss under this insurance?   ☐ Yes ☐ No

If Yes, please give details.

11 — EXPERIENCE OF ORGANISER OF EVENT

a) How many Events of this type has organiser organised?   ☐ Events

b) How many years has the organiser operated under the present name?   ☐ years

12 — COVER REQUESTED (Subject to acceptability)

CANCELLATION OR ABANDONMENT
Please refer to the brief summary of cover for guidance
☐ ESSENTIAL   ☐ SUPERIOR   ☐ SUPERIOR PLUS

FAILURE TO VACATE
Is the limit adequate?   ☐ Yes ☐ No
If No, please state sum insured required   £ _____

LIQUIDATED DAMAGES (a penalty imposed on you)
Are you responsible under your contract with your Venue(s) for liquidated damages?   ☐ Yes ☐ No
If Yes, please state amount of penalty   £ _____

ALL RISKS INSURANCE
Will the total value of your own property plus property for which you are responsible exceed £25,000?   ☐ Yes ☐ No
If Yes, please state full value   £ _____

LEGAL LIABILITIES
Please indicate the Public Liability limit required
☐ £1 Million   ☐ £2 Million   ☐ £5 Million   ☐ £10 Million

Do you have existing annual Employers Liability and Public Liability insurances?   ☐ Yes ☐ No

TRAVEL INSURANCE
Do you require cover for travel insurance?   ☐ Yes ☐ No
If Yes, please state the estimated number of:

a) Your own staff and officials   ☐

b) Delegates or official guests   ☐

c) If more than *100 persons* travel on the same aircraft state number?   ☐

PLEASE READ BELOW AND SIGN

Signing this Proposal Form does not bind the applicant or underwriters to complete the insurance, but it is agreed that this proposal shall be incorporated into and form part of any policy issued in respect of the Event specified.
I declare that the statements and estimates made herein after due inquiry are true to the best of my knowledge and belief.

Name _____

Signature _____
(as authorised person for and on behalf of insured)

Title _____   Date _____
If the Event is organised by an independent organiser on behalf of the insured the following is to be completed
ORGANISER (if different from insured)
I declare that the statements and estimates herein are made after due enquiry of my client and are true to the best of my knowledge and belief

Name of Organiser _____

Name of Contact _____

Signature _____ date _____
(as authorised person for and on behalf of organiser)

Payment may be made by bankers direct wire transfer to **BARCLAYS BANK PLC, 73/75, Calverley Road, Tunbridge Wells, Kent TN1 2UZ**
NB Banks charge for transfers so ensure we receive the full total premium net after charges
for Insurex Limited A/C No. **30061093**   (Sort Code) **20-88-13**   Date transfer arranged — insert here _____

Card Number ☐☐☐☐☐☐☐☐☐☐☐☐☐☐☐☐

INSUREX ARE PLEASED TO ACCEPT PAYMENT BY: *VISA* MasterCard €
Name on Card _____

Signature _____   Expiry Date ___ / ___   Tick Card as appropriate

Figure 9.5   Insurance plan (concluded)

by membership of professional associations. Check, too, their adherence to codes of conduct. Should you also obtain references from banks or other traders?

Sound knowledge and experience   Of their field, goods and services *and* the conference industry, if possible, so they can do the job they are employed to do, and do it well? So they know what works *and* what does not, and have dealt with most problems before and can avoid them this time? You can verify this through trade body membership. Check their years in business, the backgrounds of key personnel and take up references as well from former and existing customers.

Interest in your requirements, and keenness to fulfil them   Are they demanding to know all about your company and the event and how they fit into it? Asking about the procedures they should follow, the people they should consult, showing a real commitment to doing a good job and to playing their part in staging a first-class conference? Can you see the evidence of this in your personal dealings with them?

Competitive prices   Are these fair and reasonable? What is the hourly rate, daily rate, cost plus modest profit? Are these in line with what you would pay elsewhere? Are you being overcharged because you are inexperienced, notably in this area? Alternatively, is this a value-for-money deal? Find out by comparing them with their rivals.

Should you build up a contacts list of possible outside suppliers who meet your requirements? How? Through whom?

You   Do you already have individuals and organizations in mind? Those with which you work at the moment on a daily, regular or occasional basis?

Your immediate colleagues   Can they make suggestions? Can anyone higher up in your company put forward names – maybe someone in purchasing, marketing or other departments?

Your business associates   Do those people and firms you do business with know of first-rate, would-be suppliers? Can the sponsors of the conference help at all? Friends, relatives, even – have they any ideas?

Others   The local tourist board? The nearest convention bureau? If they cannot offer practical help themselves they may know of other suppliers who can. Can you seek advice from trade bodies – your own or suppliers' representative associations, such as the British Printing Industries Federation, for example? (Check out the *Directory of British Associations* in your local library – this lists more than 6,500 of these bodies. Also, refer to 'Reference Tools' on page 215.)

Alternative methods How about adding to your list by referring to inserts in trade directories – *Conferences and Exhibitions Diary* most obviously? Advertisements in appropriate publications such as *Conference and Exhibition Fact Finder*, and *Conference and Seminar Selector-Pack* too? (See 'Reference Tools' on page 215.)

Can you negotiate successfully with outside individuals and organizations? How? What should you do?

Approach at least three prospective suppliers of each facility or service – ideally, those who appear, from your own knowledge or on the basis of others' recommendations, to meet your criteria. Less than three is not sufficient to compare and contrast; more than three may prove unnecessarily time-consuming.

Meet with the suppliers and tell them, in as much detail as possible, what you want. Explain their tasks and duties, how and when these should be carried out and how they fit into the overall pattern of your firm and the event. State also how much you are willing to pay. The more information you can give the better, so that ideas may be properly formulated and valid suggestions made.

Find out as much about them as you can. Do they really fulfil your requirements? Do they have conflicting interests? Are they working for your closest rivals perhaps? When did they begin trading? How long have their key personnel been in the industry? Are they members of their professional association? When did they join? Are they recognized by other bodies? Do they seem keen – asking you for more details, for example? Do their prices appear fair and reasonable?

Listen to their ideas and suggestions. Is their advice impartial? Is it good? Is it practical with regard to transport and security, maybe, and creative in relation to decorating the venue? Are they stylish in their approach to catering and social activities? Look at their work, both past and present commitments. Is it top-notch quality? What do you think of the staff? Do you get on well with them?

Obtain references from their previous customers, by telephone rather than letter, for off-the-record comments. Did they act in a professional manner? Did they do a good job, on time and at the agreed price? Are there any complaints and, if so, what? Ask if they would use them again. Take up bank and trade references too, particularly if money is being handed over in advance. Can you do this through your own bank?

Choose a supplier for each specific task and duty. Which of the three is most reputable and trustworthy, has the most appropriate knowledge and experience, is really interested, has the keenest prices, and so on? Detail any agreements in writing – play safe! Reject the remaining individuals and organizations as politely as possible – you may need them on some future occasion!

Can you work well with your chosen suppliers? How can you achieve this?

Keep in touch with them from start to finish through ongoing weekly or fortnightly contact. Use the phone and obtain updates by fax. Always be available or return calls promptly, at the earliest opportunity. Answer queries and tackle problems there and then, rather than putting them off until later.

Do what you say you will do, and on time. Read the proofs of publicity material and return them with corrected errors within the agreed period. Provide the insurers of the conference with a copy of your existing policy, as promised. In short – be reliable!

Check they are doing what they have ageed to do, and at the right time. Are those signs ready to be seen? The banners? The sashes? If not, why not? Do this on a regular and discreet basis.

Notify changes at the earliest opportunity. This applies to the finalized programme, business activities, social activities, and any change of speaker. These may necessitate a new collection point or different timings, for example. Try to keep changes to a minimum to restrain costs. If, say, more signs are needed unexpectedly, if a different design is required or prices increase, put any amendments in writing to avoid subsequent disagreements.

Recommended reading

Fisher, R., Ury, W. and Patton, B. (1994), *Getting to Yes*, Random House, London.
Hodgson, J. (1994), *Thinking on Your Feet in Negotiations*, Pitman, London.

Kennedy, G. (1994), *The Perfect Negotiation*, Random House, London.
Ury, W. (1994), *Getting Past No*, Random House, London.

10

Speaking in Public

Almost inevitably, you will not only be expected to organize a success-ful conference but also to play an active role in it – typically, making an opening speech, introducing speakers and sessions and rounding off the event with a closing speech as well. You might also have to stand in for speakers if any of them withdraw at the very last moment. Thus you need to take an overview of what you are (or might be) expected to do and then prepare and rehearse what you are going to say so that you are able to make a winning speech, lead a constructive discussion, or do whatever else is required.

Taking an overview

To begin with, stand back and take a broad overview of what you are likely to have to do at the conference. Have a clear idea of what's what before proceeding any further. As important, always be prepared for the unexpected – there have been many occasions when a speaker has arrived late (or not at all!) and the organizer has had to step in to run a session with little or no notice. Make certain you are ready for such a situation.

Why are you speaking?

Is it to open the conference, to welcome speakers, delegates and their partners? Or are you making a speech or presentation on a given topic, perhaps to put across details about recent sales figures? Are you speaking in your own right or as a first reserve?

Are you chairing a discussion, about reaching a trade agreement, perhaps? Is your speech combined with a question-and-answer session? Are you chairing a panel taking questions from the floor? Is this a definite commitment or are you on stand-by?

Are you speaking as part of a demonstration to show how a new machine is operated, the benefits of using it and how to make the most of it? Will you definitely be doing this or only if someone else is unavailable?

Are you acting as a link, thanking the last speaker and introducing the next, or announcing a break for coffee, lunch or tea?

Are you closing the event, summarizing the programme and bidding farewell to speakers, delegates and their partners?

What do you want to achieve? What is your general aim? Your specific objectives?

The opening speech   Are you speaking to put everyone at their ease, to make sure they know what is happening and when, by greeting them warmly and telling them about the different activities planned, where and when they will take place and who they should approach with queries?

The speech or presentation   Is this about sales figures? To motivate delegates to work harder and better? To maintain or improve their performance by reviewing sales figures, identifying problem areas, proposing, discussing and agreeing solutions and setting new targets, perhaps?

The discussion   Is the question-and-answer session about a trade agreement, to agree on a unified approach to universal problems by highlighting changing circumstances, causes and effects, suggesting and debating remedies and settling on common solutions?

The demonstration   Is this to demonstrate that new piece of machinery and how to operate it, to retrain delegates and to maximize their work-rate and performance as quickly as possible by showing how the machine works, how it differs from old machinery and how to use it effectively? Will you give delegates the chance to practise with it?

As a link   Is the purpose to move the programme on as smoothly and as quickly as possible and ensure everyone knows what is happening by acknowledging what has just gone and explaining briefly what is coming next?

The closing speech   Is its aim to make everyone feel positive about the event by highlighting the theme and key points again, thanking every-body and explaining what happens next and how they will benefit from it?

Who is your audience?

Is it an in-house crowd? Do you know them all – the influential ones and the others? Are you familiar with the dynamics of the group, how its members mix together and the relationships, and tensions. What are you facing – a jokey, friendly atmosphere? A welcoming one? Are they all unknown to you? Do they know each other? If so, will *you* feel as though you are an outsider, excluded from a close-knit group? If not, will you be entering a rather nervous and expectant group, slightly unsure about the situation, and will this help you to take control?

What is their level of knowledge, experience and expertise? Is this specific group familiar with your trade or industry, conversant with technical data and jargon? Will they feel patronized if you don't use such phrases? Is it a more generalized audience, alienated by specialist language and requiring simple, straightforward words and explana-tions?

How many will you be facing? Up to a dozen, perhaps, which favours an informal, sitting-on-the-edge-of-a-desk style with you smiling and talking to each person in turn. Up to thirty? You will need to take a slightly more formal approach, standing up in order to be seen but still maintaining plenty of personal contact? More than thirty will require a rather more formal, distant and detached relation-ship.

What do your audience want from you?

The opening speech   Do they have similar objectives to you – to be relaxed, to be told about the forthcoming activities? Or do they want you to shut up so they can go for a coffee, meet up with old friends or go straight into the first session?

The speech or presentation   What do they want from this? Information only? Advice? Guidance? The opportunity to ask questions? Do they wish to have some input into it, even? How do their objectives differ from yours?

The discussion   At the question-and-answer session, do they want to hear your viewpoint, perhaps? To listen to what others have to say? To be given the opportunity to make comments as well?

The demonstration   What are their wants and needs here? To see a new product, perhaps for the first time? To watch it being operated or in action? To examine it for themselves? To question you about it?

The link   Do they want you to acknowledge what has just gone and ex-plain what is coming next? Possibly not! Perhaps they would rather hear the speaker now, go for lunch immediately or to the toilet even!

The closing speech   Are their objectives rather similar to your own – to be thanked, to be reminded about what happens next, or do they want to leave straightaway so that they can arrive home as early as possible?

For how long are you expected to speak?

Are you speaking only briefly, linking one session to another in just a few moments, introducing the conference to everyone or drawing the event to a close, over perhaps five minutes at most?

Perhaps you are speaking for longer? Giving a ten- or fifteen-minute demonstration, or a speech or presentation lasting for 30 minutes? Maybe the session is much longer – a 45-minute discussion or even as much as an hour if followed by questions and answers?

Is the time set aside acceptable? Is it too short? Will you need more than ten minutes to demonstrate a new product and explain its revised features and so on? Is it too long? Will you require less than 45 minutes to discuss regional sales figures to date, identify the problems, and so forth? Most important at this stage, is the time available flexible? Make sure the answer is 'yes'!

How does your speech fit into the programme?

Is it at the beginning, midway through or at the end? More impor-tantly, do you know what is being covered before, alongside *and* after your speech? Can you complement what fellow speakers have to say rather than pre-empting them, repeating their comments and contra-dicting them? Liaise, so that you present a unified image!

Does your speech also reflect the theme of your conference (for example, to work hard and well or to reach an agreement)? Can it do this subtly, as and where appropriate, without endlessly repeating the theme so the audience becomes sick and tired of it?

Whereabouts will you speak?

You have picked a good venue, but consider it again with regard to what *you* have to do. Is it somewhere informal or formal? A small room, set aside for a hands-on discussion or a large hall, suited to important speeches? Are you speaking in the right place? Will you be sitting on a chair facing a semi-circle of seated delegates? Will you be standing before them, behind a table or from a platform? Behind a podium, maybe?

Will you be speaking with or without equipment? With visual aids? With a flip-chart, perhaps, or an overhead projector? With audio-visual aids? Slides, with sound? A video? A film with a running sound commentary? What is available to you?

Preparing to speak

Mindful of your answers to all these background questions, you can then move on to prepare for what you are going to say in an opening speech, or link.

Can you sketch out a loose, provisional framework for your speech? What should you include?

For an opening speech Are you welcoming speakers, delegates and partners and thanking them for coming? Mentioning times and places of forthcoming business and social activities and referring delegates to a timetable, perhaps? Will you comment on the venue and overnight accommodation, the facilities and services and where to go for assistance? Are you inviting them to socialize for coffee or lunch and telling them what time they should reassemble?

For a speech or presentation on a specific subject Say what you are going to cover and in what order. Tell them about the equipment you will use and for how long you will talk. Work through the subject in three to six sections, perhaps. Summarize what it was that you covered. Throw the subject open to debate?

For a discussion   Will you have a question-and-answer session, too? Introduce those who are involved and thank everyone for coming? Have opening statements in turn? Give an opportunity for others to expand on, add to or question earlier statements? Allow a round of applause? Throw the session open to the floor? Take questions in turn? Answers? Conclusion? (Agree to disagree!) Thank all for their attendance, and comments? Lead a final round of applause?

For a demonstration   Display any relevant equipment, machinery or products for all to see. Pause for effect? Describe any items, pointing out various features. Give a practical demonstration of how it works, stressing the benefits as you go along. Will you offer delegates a chance to examine and use it and give them the opportunity to ask questions?

For a link   Thank the speaker warmly, highlighting one or two of the most important points again. Encourage another round of applause. Introduce the next person to speak. Outline his or her background and expertise, referring to what they are going to talk about. Lead a further round of applause as you stand down.

A closing speech   Thank speakers, delegates and partners for attending. Summarize the main findings of the event. Thank the personnel at the venue and overnight accommodation, and others who helped. Initiate a round of applause, as appropriate. Mention what happens next – copies of a conference report to be sent out shortly? Any further information? Time and place of next event? Bid them farewell. A final round of applause – hopefully for you!

Are you then able to fill out the various points within the framework? Build up a solid speech?

For that opening speech   Welcome speakers by name, especially guest speakers from outside your firm. Refer to delegates more generally, by company, perhaps? Give a special mention to partners to show they are valued. Which particular activities should be spoken about? All? Time-consuming and boring? Some? The key ones for speakers and delegates and the most interesting for partners? How about the venue and overnight accommodation? The facilities and services available free of charge and those that are not? What else?

Concerning that speech or presentation on a given topic   What exactly are you going to cover and in what order? What equipment will you use? How long will you talk for? What will comprise each section – explanation, examples, supporting material? On a flip-chart, perhaps? Should you include a joke or an anecdote? The conclusion? Anything else?

Regarding the discussion or question-and-answer session   Introduce people by their preferred names (check to find out what these are). Thank everyone personally – by name or more generally? By firm? What statements will be made, by whom and in what sequence? What will be the contents of these statements? Find the answers and coordinate everything before the session. What questions might be asked? Anticipate them in advance and work out answers. Allocate questions and answers to those who are best equipped to handle them!

Relating to a demonstration   What equipment, machinery and products are you going to display? How will you describe them? Which features will you point out? How will you demonstrate items? Have you successfully operated them yourself? What types of questions might be raised? What will your prepared responses be?

With regard to a link   Thank the speaker by name. Which are the most significant points you should reiterate? Check with the speaker beforehand and/or look at the script if available. Find out how the following speaker likes to be introduced. What should be said about his or her background, expertise and imminent speech? Again, ask and refer to a script, as and where appropriate.

For that closing speech   Who should you thank? Everyone generally? Speakers, by name? Delegates, by firm? Partners, too? What are the main findings? Can you predict them beforehand? Which personnel should you thank? All in general? Some specifically and others more generally? What else? Main points such as reports or the next conference? Minor points such as reminding people to take all their belongings with them, otherwise these will be kept at the venue, forwarded to head office or whatever?

What should you then do with all your accumulated notes? Should you make a speech with or without notes? What are the alternatives? Their pros and cons?

Speaking without notes   Does this look impressive and show you are knowledgeable and competent? Does it inspire confidence and admiration, even? However, delegates may remember your ability to speak freely, rather than what you actually said. Also, can you do it well?

How long is your speech? How much do you have to remember and cover? How experienced are you? Are you facing a sympathetic or a demanding audience? Do you *need* to do it without notes? Why?

With brief notes   On postcards or even an envelope so that they are compact, easy to hold and refer to? While they may provide support and boost confidence, they are tricky to write. You need enough notes to act as a reminder but not so many that you become dependent on them.

Using other notes   On a flip-chart? On an overhead projector? The same notes that the audience has to write down for later reference? The advantages are that they are a good support and are simple to look at (making it easy to create the impression that you are talking without notes!). Are such notes suitable for you and the audience, though? Are they too detailed for you and too brief for them? Are you too dependent? Are they too distracting? A good choice? Probably not!

With a full script   Everything you say word for word? Each word? Every pause? As an aid in organizing your thoughts beforehand? It may be acceptable for a very short 'on-the-record' speech, but can sound unnatural. Your speech may be stilted and you could miss your place, too. Will you lose contact with the audience? Is a prepared script inflexible? All in all, it is not a wise idea!

Rehearsing your speech

It is vitally important that you rehearse thoroughly what you are going to say. Whatever you expect to have to do, practice makes perfect – or at least much better.

How and where should you rehearse?

Out loud? It is possible to rehearse a speech in your head but it doesn't work! In the privacy of your office or home to begin with? In front of a mirror? Possibly, although you will concentrate less on your speech and more on you. In front of a camcorder if one is available? A better idea! You can focus on your speech and assess it and your performance later on.

In front of other people – colleagues, perhaps, who know the subject well and are experienced speakers themselves and can offer constructive advice and suggestions? Family and friends, even, who can comment on your general performance and give an honest opinion, without fear or favour? At the venue itself so you can practise with the equipment you will be handling on the day and judge how it all comes together in the actual environment?

Which aspects of the speech should you check and amend?

The contents   Does it have a good framework? Is it well structured? All in the right order? Is it logical? Does it flow easily from one point to another? Are all the points relevant and interesting? Are you completely happy with the contents?

The style   Does it have the right style? An appropriate one for the circumstances? Clear and concise words, sentences and phrases? Is it easy to understand and absorb? What about some dash – flair, even? Fresh, spot-on jokes? Impressive statements? Wry and amusing comments, if relevant?

The equipment being used   Will you be using visual aids, such as a flipchart? Audio-visual aids such as slides with a separate sound track? Do these fit in well and allow you to move smoothly from your speech to the equipment and back again? Can you handle them properly without errors or mishaps?

The length   Does it finish at the right time or thereabouts? Is it too short, perhaps? Should you expand certain points, still keeping them relevant and interesting and avoiding waffle? Should you add points – an example or another anecdote? Is it too long? Should you speed up? Would you end up gabbling your speech if you did? Should you wait? (Yes!) If your speech is trim and tidy and still too long, ask for more time to talk.

What about you as a speaker? Which are the key areas of concern here?

Your appearance   Should you choose formal attire, be smartly dressed or smart but casual? Which is right in the circumstances? Make the correct choice, otherwise you will feel self-conscious and ill-at-ease. Be comfortable, too. A new shirt with an itchy collar, a jacket which is thick and heavy, trousers which are rather tight or pinching shoes will all hinder your performance.

Facial expressions   Can the audience see your face? If so, one expression says more than a hundred words – a frown when reading out unsatisfactory sales figures, or a smile when commenting on the success of a particular salesperson's activities. Make certain that your expressions match what you are trying to say: 'Work harder' requires a different facial expression to 'Well done' and so on. Use expressions to emphasize points and drive them home to your audience.

Your voice   Make sure you can be heard. Speak out and hold up your head. Open your mouth wide. Have you a good, strong voice? Vary it to maintain the audience's interest. Use a faster pace to convey urgency, and a slower one to emphasize a point. Pauses, for effect? Higher pitch to show enthusiasm and lower to stress a comment? A quieter voice, even, to indicate the importance of what you are saying?

Eye contact   Whenever possible, maintain eye-to-eye contact with the audience to attract and hold attention, obtain feedback and build rapport. Look around on a regular basis, though, giving equal attention to all unless you are speaking specifically to one person who should receive your undivided attention. Stay attentive at all times!

Your body language   Be well placed so that everyone can see you. Can you also read your notes, see that flip-chart, overhead projector or whatever without obscuring them? Standing, to be seen, shows respect for your audience and creates a more impressive image of you and what you have to say. You are more easily heard when you are standing, too. Sitting down is more informal and friendly and increases audience participation. Keep relatively still with your hands on the overhead projector, perhaps, or holding your notes. Occasional, planned movements can be effective – the jabbing finger to emphasize a point, the sweep of an arm towards a new product. Avoid wild and excessive movements, waving arms and striding to and fro (they make you look nervous, and distract and unsettle the audience). Steer clear of repetitive and annoying mannerisms such as tapping your feet or jangling your keys.

Your nerves   Are you tense, nervous, yet rather excited? Can you imagine handling the audience well? Being applauded? Is it a nice feeling? Nerves are normal and helpful, too! The adrenalin flows, warming you up for the performance. Why worry? Haven't you done everything you can possibly do? Taken an overview? Prepared to speak? Rehearsed thoroughly? Are you ready to succeed?

Recommended reading

Forsyth, P. (1994), *Readymade Activities for Presentation Skills*, Pitman, London.

Jay, A. (1993), *Effective Presentation*, Pitman, London.

Mandel, S. (1993), *Effective Presentation Skills*, Kogan Page, London.

Watson, W., Pardo, L., and Tomovic, V. (1994), *How to Give an Effective Seminar*, Kogan Page, London.

11

Using Equipment

If you are expected to make a speech, chair a discussion, or what-ever, you will need to have some knowledge of the equipment you might use during the programme. Even if you are not involved in this capacity, you need an understanding of the types of equipment available as speakers may turn to you for help and advice at some stage. You should think about including visual and audio-visual aids in the conference and know how to make the most of any equipment used.

Including visual aids

There are many visual aids which you may choose to include in your event either for you or other speakers to use, as and when required.

Have you considered product displays? Set up by those outsiders decorating the venue on your behalf?

Their main advantage is that they give delegates the chance to see, touch and even taste what you are talking about – all of which helps to create a powerful and lasting impression. What else?

What about their disadvantages? Are they difficult or too expensive to transport? Are they too large and bulky for the venue or perhaps too heavy to be supported? Anything else?

Are there any similar alternatives, such as models of buildings, equipment or machinery? Are there samples available of materials used in a particular process or component parts of a machine? What are the advantages and disadvantages of these? Are they easy to examine – can you gain an instant impression? What is the cost of models? Are the samples unrepresentative?

Have you thought about flip-charts?

Advice on using flip-charts is provided in Figure 11.1 below. Their positive features are that they are inexpensive, informal, intimate and useful for putting across detailed information to a small and friendly group of delegates. Are there any other positive features?

How about their negative features? They have an amateurish feel and give a rather low-key impression. Nor are they so good in formal situations or with larger groups. What other negative features do they have?

What are the comparable alternatives? Blackboards with white and coloured chalks? Whiteboards with special marker pens? What are their positive and negative features? Are the alternatives cost effective and easy to use? Might they be messy, though, and difficult to clean?

☐ Use a flip-chart only if it is clearly visible to everybody in the room

☐ Make sure the stand is stable and will not fall over

☐ Score pages to be torn off before you begin – to save a struggle later on!

☐ Pencil in headings and drawings too – make it easy on yourself!

☐ Have spare paper and marker pens to hand just in case

☐ Stand well clear of the flip-chart while you speak

☐ Write in large letters, and avoid writing *and* talking at the same time – always a recipe for disaster!

☐ Show each page for at least one minute, giving everyone time to note its contents

☐ Tear off pages as and when you move on, but not before the audience has finished making notes

---

Figure 11.1   Flip-charts: a checklist

How about overhead projectors? What do you think of them?

You will find detailed guidance for using these aids in Figure 11.2 below.

Their pluses are that they are cheap to use, down-to-earth and unpretentious. They may be most suited to small numbers of in-house delegates. Are there other plus points?

Their minuses include their rather basic, even unprofessional, image. They can be tricky to use and are less suitable with larger numbers of outsiders expecting an upmarket, classy presentation. Are there more minus points?

☐ Ensure that the transparency can be seen by making it as large as you can and by cleaning the surface and lens of the overhead projector thoroughly beforehand

☐ Understand how to use the projector, fit a replacement bulb if necessary – and put in the transparencies the correct way up

☐ Use prepared and tested transparencies so you know that they fit properly and can be seen clearly and fully – top to bottom, left to right

☐ Number transparencies, if appropriate

☐ Dim the lights and/or close the curtains, if necessary

☐ Stand away from the overhead projector as you talk

☐ Give the audience time to read what is on the screen. Don't talk as they read. NEVER repeat what they can see for themselves

☐ Turn off the projector when you go on to the next stage of your speech and when the audience have finished looking at the screen

---

Figure 11.2 Overhead projectors: a checklist

How about slides? A straightforward slide-show projected on to a wall or a screen?

General guidance on slide-shows is given in Figure 11.3 on page 176.

The pros? They are vivid, colourful and therefore memorable. They give a professional, polished image and are seen by many people. What else?

The cons? They are costly and prone to errors – slides may be in the

☐ Use a screen which is as large as possible, so that everyone can see

☐ Be familiar with the projector, controls and how to operate them, if relevant

☐ Check that slides are in the correct sequence and position

☐ Number slides if necessary

☐ Dim the lights to focus attention on the screen

☐ Say what is going to be shown

☐ Only speak at the rehearsed moments – never become carried away

☐ Try not to talk too much. Let the picture do that for you

☐ Switch off the projector as soon as the last slide has been studied

☐ Pause before recommencing your speech to allow the audience time to return their attention to you

Figure 11.3 Slides: a checklist

wrong order, back to front or upside-down. They can be fiddly to operate and are unsuitable for in-depth details needing to be shown in a darkened room, which reduces speaker–delegate contact. Any others?

Have you thought about using handouts? Perhaps summarizing the key points of a speech?

Using handouts is looked at in more detail in Figure 11.4 on page 177.

What are their good points? Are they cheap and easy to produce and full of detailed facts and figures? Do they enable delegates to listen attentively to a speech rather than make notes? Can they be retained for later reference? Is that it?

Do they have any bad points? A 'college lecture' image, possibly? Are they rather rough and ready? Do they encourage delegates to read rather than listen to a speaker? If held back until the end of a speech, will delegates then start making notes during the speech? (Yes!) Are there more bad points?

Incorporating audio-visual aids

Equally there are numerous audio-visual aids which could be incorpo-

---

☐ **Provide A4 rather than A5 paper which makes text look small and cramped**

☐ **Check for spelling mistakes and grammatical errors which reflect badly on your professionalism**

☐ **Make sure that text is clear and readable – retype and photocopy again if necessary**

☐ **Staple pages together so that second and third sheets are less likely to be mislaid, but number pages as well, just in case**

☐ **Have spare copies to hand, as some of the originals will inevitably be lost**

☐ **Distribute handouts at the end of each session – earlier than that and delegates may be distracted from your speech**

☐ **Allow delegates time to study the handouts before going on**

☐ **Avoid the urge to read out the notes for them – let delegates do it for themselves**

Figure 11.4   Handouts: a checklist

rated in the event, either for your own or other speakers' use, as appropriate.

Have you considered slides with sound? With a running commentary prepared in-house or by outside specialists?

Tips on adding sound to slide-shows are set out in Figure 11.5 on page 178.

What are the advantages of slides with sound? Are they striking, bright, memorable, classy? Can they be seen and heard by many delegates? Do they give you the opportunity to record the perfect speech in the right voice, pace and style and without coughs, hesitations and mistakes? What are their other advantages?

How about the disadvantages? Will you incur more expense, especially if an outside specialist is used? Is there an increased chance of errors? Might there be difficulty in synchronizing audio and visual elements in particular – with embarrassing consequences? Could this convey a sloppy, unprofessional image? What are the other disadvantages?

☐ Have a screen which is big enough to be seen by everbody in the room – sitting or standing

☐ Be able to handle the projector and its controls if necessary

☐ Make certain that slides are where they should be – in the right order and position

☐ Number slides in case of an emergency – they may be knocked on to the floor!

☐ Reduce the lighting levels as necessary

☐ Tell the audience what is happening

☐ Step back, watch and listen. Be ready to move in if sound and vision are not synchronized perfectly. Act quickly *before* the audience starts to complain or laugh

☐ Turn off the sound if you can, reading from a script if required. Do not abandon the show!

☐ Switch off the projector promptly at the end of the sequence

☐ Allow the audience time to absorb any information given before proceeding with the session

Figure 11.5   Slides with sound: a checklist

Have you thought about using films with an accompanying soundtrack?

General advice on introducing films into a conference is provided in Figure 11.6 on page 179.

What are their positive features – colour, movement, the ability to demonstrate without making mistakes, quality speech, and the incorporation of music? Do they offer a highly skilful and professional performance all round? What else is there to recommend them?

What about the negative features? Are there substantial costs involved? Will you need to bring in outside help, and thus lose some control? Is there a tendency for such films to dominate the proceedings to the detriment of other speeches and presentations? Is there anything else to consider which is negative?

☐ Project the film on to a screen which can be seen by all, wherever they are in the room

☐ Be able to work the projector – if an emergency happens, everybody will probably look towards you!

☐ Turn down the lights and draw the curtains, as necessary

☐ Wet the audience's appetite for the film by telling them a little about it. Not too much though!

☐ Sit down, look and learn. Never intervene unless a problem occurs. Be especially careful not to make superfluous and repetitive comments over the soundtrack

☐ Take charge only if a difficulty arises, reading from a prepared script or whatever is appropriate. The show must go on!

☐ Turn off the projector when the film comes to an end

☐ Pause before continuing so that the audience's interest switches back to you before you begin talking!

Figure 11.6 Films: a checklist

What about videos? Are these relevant?

The use of videos at an event is detailed further in Figure 11.7 below.

☐ Only use videos if everyone can see the television screen clearly

☐ Know how to operate the television, video player and remote controls (if appropriate)

☐ Be comfortable about handling videos too

☐ Make sure the video starts where you want it to

☐ Number videos if necessary to avoid confusion

☐ To aid visibility, lower the lights and/or draw the curtains

☐ Explain briefly what the video is about before showing it

☐ Never talk over a video. Freeze the frame first

☐ Do not freeze the picture too often

☐ Turn the television and video player off as soon as the video has finished

☐ Give the audience time to gather their thoughts before you continue talking

Figure 11.7 Videos: a checklist

The pluses? Are they bright and lively, with sound, music, movement and action? Do they give a first-rate, classy image? Other plus points?

The cons? Drawbacks may include the costs of production if made especially for your firm or event. If you have outside assistance there is the expense of buying ready-made videos to consider. Videos may take over the programme and become the most remembered part of the event. Will ready-made videos have exactly the same theme and message as your conference? Probably not! Other cons?

Making the most of equipment

Once you know the main types of visual and audio-visual aids available, along with their advantages and disadvantages, be aware of how to maximize their effectiveness as far as possible. Various points need to be addressed.

What are the benefits of using aids? Why should they be included in a speech or a discussion?

Perhaps they help to put across a message better. Does a product display have a greater impact than a verbal description of those goods? Do vivid and colourful charts of statistics on an OHP screen have a more powerful effect than simply reading out sets of figures?

Do they save time – your time? Does a slide sum up in one second what would take you five minutes to explain? Does it save delegates' time? Do handouts enable delegates to listen rather than make notes about what you are saying?

Do they add variety and style to a speech? Do colour, sound, movement, action and so on seize attention, maintain interest and enthusiasm in the message being put over?

Do they help the audience to retain a message for longer? Are delegates more likely to recall that handled product than a brief description of it? Will the contents of a film or video be remembered long after a straightforward speech has been forgotten?

What are the drawbacks to using aids?

Do they take considerable time, effort and money to arrange? Think carefully whether you should use them or not. Which aids will you use? Should you hire or buy outright? Where do you obtain them – in-house, at the venue or from outside suppliers? Who transports them to the venue and how? Do you hire a technician, and if so from where?

Are aids sometimes irrelevant and unnecessary, brought in because they are expected by the audience or used because other speakers incorporate them in their speeches? Might they be included as a gimmick or to fill out a programme?

Are they occasionally difficult to handle properly? Bulbs sometimes fail in an overhead projector, slides get out of sequence. Sound and vision may become unsynchronized. Video players may fail to rewind or chew up the tape (most likely because of speakers trying to operate them with thumbs but no fingers!).

Do they often dominate the whole programme? Are preceding sessions ill-attended or sat through reluctantly while delegates wait for the film to begin? Do subsequent sessions suffer because delegates are still thinking about the exciting video they have just seen? Looking back, do delegates remember the gadgetry, the music and the glitz rather than the message?

What aids should you use in your particular circumstances? What are the main influences on your decision?

The audience   Is it a small or a large group? For example, will members of a larger audience all be able to read notes on a flip-chart? Are handouts better? Is it an informal or a formal audience of in-house or outside delegates? Will a formal group be impressed when faced with an overhead projector? If not, slides may be more appropriate.

The message   Is it a pep talk, for example, or a motivating speech? Does that actually need a visual or an audio-visual aid? Why? Is it an informative message with a substantial amount of basic information to convey? Does this suggest the use of handouts?

The speaker   What do you and the other speakers feel is most relevant for each particular session? Perhaps you consider that a product display is important when you are speaking about new goods. Do fellow speakers want graphs and charts displayed on screen while they are talking about sales figures?

The budget   What can you afford? How much have you set aside for visual and audio-visual aids? Do you have the money to bring in outside help, to pay for specialist assistance and produce quality films and videos? Should you spend beyond your means? Certainly not!

What are the dos and don'ts of using equipment properly?

Prepare thoroughly! Practise with the equipment when you are rehearsing your speech so that you know how to operate it competently and can introduce it effortlessly, without hesitation or delay. Can you develop a smooth and effective style so that aids blend into your performance?

Don't use complex equipment. Stay within your capabilities and avoid equipment which you find difficult to handle well. Failing this, employ a technician to deal with the equipment on your behalf and have him or her at rehearsals so that visual and audio-visual aids can be integrated into your speech.

Check, double check and check the equipment yet again before using it. Make certain that it works and is not about to break down – invariably at the worst possible moment. Don't become too dependent on it, just in case it does fail. Have a bag of spares, such as pens for the flip-chart and bulbs for the overhead projector, available to remedy any problems which occur. See Figure 11.8 below for a list of useful spares.

☐ Batteries	☐ Paper (carbon, flip-chart, hand-out)
☐ Blu-tack	
☐ Bulbs	☐ Pencils
☐ Correction fluid	☐ Pens (ballpoint, felt-tipped, marker)
☐ Dusters	☐ Pins (coloured, safety)
☐ Fuses	☐ Scissors
☐ Glue	☐ Sellotape
☐ Knives	☐ Transparencies
☐ Masking tape	☐ What else?

Figure 11.8 Useful spares: a checklist

Don't forget that these are aids, not substitutes. They should help to support and substantiate your message, not replace it. Never use them simply for the sake of it, as a gimmick or to jazz up a faltering speech. Never allow them to take over, blur your message or detract from it. Stay in control!

Recommended reading

Crofts, A. (1993), *Using Television and Video in Business*, Management Books 2000, Didcot.

Flegg, D. and McHale, J. (1991), *Selecting and Using Training Aids*, Kogan Page, London.

Nicolay, C. and Barrette, J. (1992), *Assembling Course Materials*, Kogan Page, London.

12

Staging Rehearsals

Even though you drafted your programme at an early stage and subsequently finalized details and checked all was well leading up to the conference, you should still stage full rehearsals perhaps a day, a week, a fortnight or whatever before the event begins. These will help you to spot and eliminate weaknesses in advance, thus improving the conference itself. To stage rehearsals successfully you need to coordinate everyone, supervise activities and make any last-minute changes that are required.

Coordinating everyone

Gathering everyone and everything together for rehearsals may seem to be nearly as complicated and time-consuming as doing it for the actual conference – but it is worthwhile if it allows you to avoid mishaps and mistakes which might otherwise damage or destroy your firm's reputation if they occurred at the event. Various individuals and organizations may need to be coordinated for this.

Will all the speakers attend rehearsals?

If they will, do they know precisely when and where they are supposed to turn up and what they have to do while they are there? Have travel and accommodation arrangements been made to ensure they arrive on time, feeling relaxed, and to enable them to stay over, if necessary? Anything else?

If not, why not? Are they unavailable? Do they not want to come? Can you persuade them to attend (by paying more, maybe?) to ensure that you can run full and complete rehearsals? If not, can you observe them practising at another time and place? If so, when and where? Can you or others stand in for them at rehearsals, using their scripts, so that the rehearsals are as similar as possible to the event?

What about delegates? Who will step in for them at rehearsals?

Will it be you who sits in on sessions to judge speakers and contents? If so, check that they can be heard at the back and that the material is relevant and interesting. Will you be participating in the planned social activities to assess them and make sure they are what delegates want? Study the venue from the delegates' viewpoint. Is it roomy, comfortable and warm enough? Appraise the overnight accommodation too. Will delegates be happy staying there?

Can your colleagues assist you here, some sitting at the front to assess facial expressions, eye-to-eye contact and so forth while others raise points at a discussion or queries during a question-and-answer session? Can they check out the social programme on your behalf, look closely at the venue and give further opinions on the overnight accommodation? Be careful though – pick people who see this as a serious assessment, not a day off!

Are the rehearsals taking place at the conference venue?

If so, are you sure the conference executive and his or her staff know who is arriving for rehearsals, how many and when? Do you know exactly what you want – which rooms, when and for how long, what facilities, services and equipment? Is this all covered in your booking form or contract? If not, notify any changes by telephone immediately, following up with a letter of confirmation.

Is the venue unavailable on your chosen dates? Should you rearrange rehearsals so they can be held there, in the actual conference environment so that shortcomings can be seen now, rather than later? Should they be held elsewhere – at head office, maybe? Is this wise, or is it better to spend money on the venue so you can assess it in action? You can't afford to wait until the event to discover its weaknesses.

How about your suppliers?

Do those who are decorating parts of the venue for you know exactly what you require? Will they provide various facilities and services for the conference, such as visual aids or audio-visual equipment? Do they also know when, where and for how long? If this is not in accordance with your existing agreements check that any changes are known, acceptable and confirmed in writing.

Are any other individuals and organizations involved? (This is often overlooked.) Have you contacted security personnel to make certain that rehearsals are just as secure as the event itself? Have you told your insurers about the rehearsals – where, when and for how long they are taking place, who and what are involved? Have you arranged suitable insurance cover for this time?

Will anyone be staying in the overnight accommodation before, during or after rehearsals?

If they are, is the hotel aware of this? Do they know who and how many will be staying, when and for how long, what your requirements are including numbers and types of rooms and the facilities and services needed? Has this already been discussed, agreed and confirmed? If not, telephone immediately with details of changes, seeking written confirmation by return.

If they are not, why not? Are the rooms unavailable at that particular time? Should you hold rehearsals on a different date so you can check out the overnight accommodation at the same time in case there are problems you need to find out about before the conference? Are you trying to minimize costs and is this worthwhile? What happens if disgruntled speakers and delegates are unhappy with the accommodation?

Supervising activities

Try to stage rehearsals which are as identical as possible to the conference itself. Clearly, the more comparable they are the easier it will be for you to identify and remedy shortcomings before the event starts. When overseeing rehearsal activities, assess the following aspects in particular.

Is the business programme unfolding satisfactorily?

The speakers   Do they seem to have prepared and rehearsed thoroughly beforehand? Are the contents of the speeches logical and flowing? Is the style appropriate for the audience? Are the speakers confident in handling any equipment used? Do they give a good overall performance – suitable appearance, facial expressions, voice, eye contact and body language? No visible nerves? Are you happy with each aspect of every speaker?

The topics   Are all the key topics being covered fully – past sales figures, selling methods, future sales targets, and so on? Do they also reflect your overall theme – 'Work hard'! 'Do better!', for example. Is this being referred to regularly? Directly? Indirectly? Not so frequently that it becomes tedious and repetitive, though?

The approach   Is the right approach being taken in speeches, presentations, discussions and question-and-answer sessions? Is a speech being made when a discussion would be better? Could it be improved by the addition of a question-and-answer session?

The order   Do you feel that everything has been put together in the most relevant order – a sensible, step-by-step sequence, perhaps? Is it all clear and understandable? Should you amend the order, manoeuvring the topics so that it makes more sense and flows more easily?

The length   What about the length of each session? Is it too short to convey all the information needed, or too long to maintain interest? Is the balance between sessions about right or should it be adjusted? Should a speech be briefer, more concise and followed by some time for questions and answers, maybe? Should there be shorter breaks, or perhaps longer ones?

Does the social programme seem satisfactory?

Are you also appraising the social programme as far as possible? Or are you simply leaving it to chance, hoping it will work out well?

With regard to catering, can you organize and then monitor coffee and tea breaks, lunches and dinners, as appropriate? Check out the activities planned for partners during the business programme – inside, a visit to the bar perhaps? Outside, a trip to the shopping centre? What about activities for speakers, delegates and partners out of business hours? Will indoor activities include the use of leisure facilities and outside activities incorporate a trip to the theatre? Is everything all right?

Is the approach ideal? Are speakers, delegates and partners left to entertain themselves indoors, or are entertainments brought in for them? Have you struck a satisfactory balance? Are they left to go out on their own or have trips been laid on? Again is everything exactly right? Is it all optional, too?

What is the order of the social programme? A break to begin with followed by some time on their own, perhaps so they can please themselves? Will entertainments then be brought in? Will there be an optional visit somewhere? Should you adjust this order so that it co-ordinates better with the business programme? Or do they already work well together?

How about the length? Are the breaks too short, giving insufficient time to unwind a little? Are they too long so that everyone is meandering about, waiting for the next session? Are the partners' activities short enough for them to be free when the business programme ends but long enough to keep them amused and entertained? Are speakers', delegates' and partners' activities short so they do not overlap with the business programme or tire people, or are they long to fill out spare time?

Is the venue proving to be acceptable, as far as you can tell?

Entrances   Check heights, lengths, widths, obstructions, power points and exits. Is it really large enough to fit everyone and everything in – speakers, stands, delegates, chairs, desks and tables, product displays and visual and audio-visual aids? Do they all fit in comfortably and allow room to see and hear what's going on, to stretch out and to move in and out easily?

Lighting   Is it bright enough for the speaker to be seen, flip-charts to be read easily and notes to be written? Is it dark enough, when necessary, to focus on slides or a film? Is it sufficiently warm but cool enough when another hundred or so people turn up on the day? Is it fully adjustable in case of a sudden temperature change? Can you check the ventilation? Is there a soothing breeze or a raging hurricane? Does it actually work, and well?

Noise levels   Inside the conference buildings, are the rehearsals proceeding from beginning to end without interruptions and distractions? Outside the buildings, is it all equally quiet and non-disruptive? Are any problems simply one-offs? If all is quiet, will it remain this way for the event?

The conference executive　Is he or she really as experienced and in control as you thought? Does he or she know what can and cannot be done? Is he or she there at your shoulder, if required, making valid suggestions, advising you on your programme and inspiring confidence? Are his or her colleagues equally good?

How about the facilities and services? Are they satisfactory?

Are those provided by the venue of good quality, up to date and in a decent condition? Are they exactly what you want? Are they easy to operate and can they be used correctly – smoothly and without mistakes? Is a technician on call if needed, and are you pleased with him or her?

Are the facilities supplied by other individuals and firms available when and where required? Are they up to standard, modern, reliable, as requested, manageable and effective? Is a technician being provided by an outside supplier? Is he or she experienced, competent and acceptable to you? Does he or she do the job that you want?

What about the overnight accommodation? Are you pleased with it?

Is your initial assessment of the rooms, based on a brief visit, supported by the evidence gained from an overnight stay? Are the rooms up to scratch – clean, tidy, comfortable, luxurious even? Are they going to satisfy or perhaps impress delegates?

Can you test the facilities and services provided during the stay? This will give you a much fuller and more accurate impression than was obtained from your earlier visit. Is there sufficient space in the wardrobes (for long dresses, possibly)? Does the shower work properly? Is room service prompt, efficient and friendly? Outside the room, are the lifts reliable and suitable for disabled people? Anything else?

Making last-minute changes

Very few conferences are staged without some adjustments having been made at rehearsals or shortly thereafter. You would have to be a genius to proceed without introducing various, last-minute changes – or more likely a complete fool! In turn, think about the amendments that may need to be implemented with regard to the following areas.

Does the business programme need to be adjusted at all? In what ways?

In relation to the speakers Hesitant flow of contents, perhaps? Use notes, then, on cards or an overhead projector. Inappropriate style, maybe? Give advice about the type of audience being faced. Poor handling of the equipment possibly? Set aside more time to practise with it. Inadequate performance even? Comment on unsuitable or repetitive speech patterns and mannerisms and replace unsatisfactory speakers if necessary.

Concerning the topics covered Typically, some not dealt with fully, or at all? Expand coverage of speeches, presentations, or whatever. Edit out surplus examples, anecdotes and so on, and add on a session, perhaps cutting into a break or social activity. Others dealt with too extensively, or even repetitively? Remove excessive and repeated coverage from sessions as appropriate. Take away a session if necessary and allow a little more time for socializing, perhaps.

With regard to the approach Do you (or whoever is representing the audience) feel frustrated, angry or resentful as you sit through different sessions? Is this because you can't respond to a speaker's viewpoint and are unable to put across your opinions? Turn a speech into a discussion session or add on time for questions and answers at the end. Is it because you can't touch and examine a product that is being talked about? Incorporate a demonstration into the programme.

Relating to the order Are you or your colleagues (sitting in as the audience) receiving information which you do not understand fully? Is the information given out of context? Were the benefits of a new product described prior to an explanation of how it actually works, or forthcoming sales targets given before an outline of past figures and prevailing market conditions? Should their order be reversed?

Concerning the length Perhaps speakers stopped too soon? Did they gabble? Encourage them to relax and slow down. Did they run out of points? Remind them. Suggest they underline notes. Is insufficient detail being given? Ask them to add examples or anecdotes to personalize. Alternatively, do they overrun? Is this because they rambled? Tell them to stick to their notes. Because of constant repetition? Suggest they be aware of this habit. Just too much material? Cut examples and anecdotes, as appropriate.

How about the social programme? Do changes need to be made to it?

Amendments to catering arrangements are most frequently necessary. Feeling sleepy after that alcoholic break? Stick to soft drinks for the conference. Rather full after that sit-down lunch? Have a finger buffet on the day. Bored by the in-house entertainments laid on? Bring your own, if possible. Also bored by the external trips? Select alternatives if other people are likely to feel the same as you.

Does the approach you have adopted need changing? One extreme exists when everyone is left to themselves and there is little to do at the venue, the overnight accommodation or in the vicinity. At the other extreme is a full timetable of compulsory fun and games. The answer is probably somewhere between these two scenarios.

The order of the activities sometimes need amending. An exciting activity to begin with can mean that everyone is over-enthusiastic and unfocused during the next business session. Move it to the end! If a less interesting activity is scheduled at the close of the event when every-one just wants to go home as soon as they can, bring it to the beginning to ease delegates into the business programme!

Does the length need changing? Social activities for partners may overrun so that they are not there when a business session ends. Start them slightly earlier perhaps? Cut them a little short? Also, speakers', delegates' and partners' activities can be too lengthy and exhausting. Reduce them so they do not break into, or affect, the business pro-gramme – make sure your priorities are correct!

Are amendments going to have to be made concerning the venue? What will they be?

Any problems with entrances – heights, lengths and so on? Not enough space for everyone and everything? So what should you do? Rearrange the room? Or ask for a larger room? Sometimes there is too much space. So what is the solution? Bring delegates to the front? Partition off excess areas? Move to a smaller room, even?

What about the lighting? Too dim? Too bright? More or less light, then, using blackout curtains if necessary? Is the room rather hot or slightly cold? Make certain the heating is adjusted on the day. Is there a smell of stale cigarette smoke or a sweaty odour? You might restrict smoking to break-times and make sure that ventilation is switched on during the event. Are there any unresolvable problems? If so, find another room or venue.

What about noise levels? Are you interrupted by a member of staff with a tea trolley? Tell the conference executive that you are not to be disturbed during sessions. Put up reminder signs too, just in case. Distracted by music rehearsals next door? Check the diary to be certain this will not occur on the day. Annoyed by roadworks or a building site? Will these be finished by the time your event begins? If not, consider moving to the reserve venue.

In relation to the conference executive and his or her team? Do they have to check everything with a superior before giving the go-ahead? Can you work this way, especially if immediate decisions may need to be made during the conference? Or are his or her comments and suggestions inappropriate? If so, ignore them.

What about the facilities and services? Any adjustments here?

Are some unavailable at the venue for rehearsals but promised for the conference? (Perhaps the secretary is off sick but will be 'back in time'?) Are others in an unsatisfactory condition? (Is the fax machine continually faulty but will be 'repaired soon'?) What else?

Are some of the facilities provided by outsiders simply not up to date? Does the photocopier copy but not laminate, as promised? Perhaps, other facilities are not easy to operate? The slide projector may be fiddly and difficult to master – far more complex than was indicated by the brochure! Anything else?

So what should you do? Can you be sure that these problems will be resolved before the event begins? Should you make do with second-rate facilities and services? Do you have time to come to terms with machinery? No – not if it will affect the smooth running of the conference or harm your firm's image. Go elsewhere for secretarial assistance, another photocopier or whatever, overseeing all changes yourself rather than relying on others – they do not share your commitment! Amend any bills, as appropriate.

How about the overnight accommodation? Any changes to this?

Are the walls of the rooms so thin that you can hear every word and movement from the adjacent ones? Does that double bed sag in the middle? Will all the guests staying in that particular block be wakened at six a.m. by the sound of deliveries into the yard below? These are all negative features which you could probably discover only after a night's stay.

What about the facilities and services inside your room? Maybe the complimentary tea and coffee machines and supplies are not tidied up and replaced? Outside your room, perhaps the wrong newspaper is left by your door in the morning? All minor points, but ones which may irritate those speakers, delegates and partners who are staying over!

What is your response? Will these difficulties be corrected in time for the conference? Yes? Can you be sure? Do you want to take a chance? Could you have annoyed and edgy participants turning up for the event? Should you consider accommodating everyone elsewhere, at your second choice hotel maybe?

Recommended reading

Cusins, P. (1994), *Be a Successful Supervisor*, Kogan Page, London.
Leigh, A. (1994), *Perfect Decisions*, Random House, London.

13

Managing the Event

Having staged rehearsals successfully, you should be able to approach the conference itself with quiet optimism – by now, you have done all that you can to ensure this is a winner. To manage the event well you have to oversee various tasks and duties. Most notably: getting everyone there, watching business activities, monitoring social activities and – last but definitely not least – sending everybody home.

Getting everyone there

Your initial task is to make sure everyone arrives punctually for the conference and in a positive frame of mind, and in addition that everything is in place for them on their arrival, and thereafter.

Has everything been arranged for speakers, and their partners? Rehearsed, as far as possible? Checked? Amended? Confirmed? Just right?

Travel arrangements   Are they making their own way there? Do they know where to go? Do they have a map? Do they also know when to arrive? Do they have those pre-conference documents? Are they aware of what to do in an emergency? Are they being collected? At what time? Are they and the collectors aware of the details? Are standby arrangements in existence in case of problems such as a train strike and coach breakdown?

Accommodation   Have sufficient rooms been booked and at the right times for the correct periods? Are they the right types, too – singles? twins? doubles? family rooms, maybe? Are they in the required places? Ground floor, perhaps, to give easier access to disabled speakers and their partners, possibly? Are facilities and services available and ready as well?

Have all the necessary arrangements also been made for delegates? Partners too, if relevant? Run through, wherever possible? Looked at? Adjusted? Confirmed? Now satisfactory?

Travel   Are they coming on their own? By car, coach, train or aeroplane? Do they know all they need to know – where and when to arrive, and so on? Are they being picked up by taxi, minibus or coach? Is everyone familiar with the pick-up points and times? Do you have someone on standby in the event of difficulties? Your colleagues? Outsiders?

Accommodation arrangements   Have the right numbers and types of rooms been made available and on the correct dates? Have they been booked for the right lengths of time and are they sited where you want them to be? Have the facilities and services that were requested been provided?

What about arrangements with the venue? Have these all been rehearsed, as far as they can be? Studied? Changed? Agreed and in writing?

Concerning speakers and delegates participating in the conference, are the conference executive and his or her team aware of who is attending, the number of people who will be there, when they will be present and for how long?

With regard to your particular requirements, which conference rooms will be occupied by the participants? When exactly are they being used? How long are they being occupied? What facilities are required – where, when and for how long? What services and equipment?

Have all the appropriate arrangements been made with your suppliers?

Has everything been tested already, viewed and amended and agreed in writing? Has everything been arranged with individuals and organizations supplying those facilities and services which are unsatisfactory or unavailable at the venue itself? Translators? Interpreters, perhaps? Are they conscious of what you want and when? Do they know you want those facilities and services to be provided and for how long?

What about other outside suppliers? Do security staff know precisely where and when the conference is taking place? Do they also know just how long they need to be there and what their responsibilities are while they are at the venue? Is sufficient insurance cover in place for everyone and everything involved with the event?

How about the overnight accommodation? Has this now been checked? Adjustments made? All agreed and put in writing?

Which speakers, delegates and their respective partners are staying overnight? How do they divide up, into single rooms, twins, or doubles and family rooms? So, how many rooms are needed, what types, when and for how long? One night for some perhaps, two for others? Where? Ground floor for some, anywhere for others?

Regarding your specific needs, does the hotel know what you want to be provided for those people staying overnight? Which facilities, services, equipment and any out-of-the-ordinary needs? Are they catering for these requirements, and satisfactorily?

Watching business activities

Probably your most prominent role during the conference will be to watch the business sessions as they take place. You need to make sure that any weaknesses exposed during rehearsals have been remedied and that the activities are all as relevant and interesting as you hoped when you drafted this part of the programme. If you remain vigilant throughout the proceedings, any outstanding errors and mishaps which occur may be rectified quickly, there and then.

Are the speakers doing well? Including you?

The contents   Are they full and complete? In a sensible order? Unfolding smoothly? Are there any omissions? Should you make suggestions during the following break such as 'You missed this! Add it in here'?

Their style   Right for this particular group of delegates, or not quite? Have a quick word in the ear at the break, then, suggesting they loosen up a little and be a touch more informal?

The equipment   Is this being used successfully by the speaker and by the technician? Does a felt-tipped pen dry up as the speaker is writing on a flip-chart? Does a bulb on the overhead projector fail? Can you hand over spares immediately?

Their general performance   All fine and satisfactory? Or are they still avoiding eye-to-eye contact and gesticulating wildly at the OHP screen almost as frequently as before? Tell them to stop it at the earliest opportunity!

Are the key topics all being incorporated fully into the sessions?

As an example, at a promotional event, is technical information about a new product included, with reasons for introducing it, its strengths, main selling features and why delegates should publicize it? Any minor oversights here? Can you add something to your next link, perhaps?

Is the theme mentioned directly and on an occasional basis? Is it reflected indirectly in comments made regularly? Not mentioned enough? Can you incorporate additional comments in your upcoming speech?

Is each session being approached in the most suitable manner?

Does a speech about that new product include why it is being introduced, its qualities, unique selling points and so on? Is it supported by handouts detailing technical data? If they are too blurred, can you have them retyped and photocopied by the end of the speech? If there are not enough, can you run off more copies in time?

Does a question-and-answer session focus on why delegates should promote it, perhaps? Maybe the speaker is unable to answer one or two questions? Can you help out without making that speaker look foolish?

Is a demonstration of how the product works followed by an opportunity for delegates to examine and test it? Perhaps the speaker can't demonstrate, talk *and* answer questions all at the same time? Can you assist, as and when required?

Are the sessions now in the correct order and of the right length?

The order All straightforward and understandable? Everything flowing naturally? Is there still room for improvement? Maybe you could swap the order of the question-and-answer session with the demonstration?

The length All short and sweet, rather than long and endless? Are one or two speakers still talking too quickly? Can you signal that they should slow down? Are others speaking for too long? Can you give another signal that they are running out of time?

Monitoring social activities

It is equally likely that you will adopt a high-profile position with regard to the social programme – you obviously want to ensure that any shortcomings identified at rehearsals have been dealt with and the activities really are suited to participants and complementary to the overall business programme. Also, speakers, delegates and their partners will inevitably approach you with any problems as they arise, often expecting you to remedy them on the spot.

Are all the social activities going well?

Catering Are the reception, coffee and tea breaks, lunches, dinners and the banquet all now satisfactory? Are there minor errors? Artificial sweeteners not provided at break-times? Can you send a waiter or waitress to collect some?

Partners' activities Is everything satisfactory inside the hotel and/or conference venue and outdoors? What about occasional mishaps – if one of the partners oversleeps and misses the coach trip can one of your colleagues drive him or her to a convenient rendezvous?

Speakers', delegates' and partners' activities Is everything now acceptable indoors and outside the hotel and/or conference venue? Are there odd mistakes here and there, perhaps an insufficient number of seats booked for the theatre visit? Can you telephone and reserve one or two extra ones?

Are the different activities being approached in an appropriate manner?

Catering   Have you just noticed that only meat-filled sandwiches are served at breaks with finger snacks and soft drinks? Add others, for vegetarians. At the buffet lunch, have you just realized that most delegates have been standing during a product demonstration and examination? Bring in more seats.

The partners' activities   Are partners left to their own devices, indoors or outdoors? Are one or two wandering around, looking miserable? Suggest various in-house activities, showing them where to go and what to do. Have you arranged everything for them? Are a few partners feeling tired or ill? Can you get them back to the hotel as soon as possible, perhaps by taxi?

Activities for speakers, delegates and their partners together   Have they been left to themselves? Are some looking confused or unhappy and unsure what they should do? Recommend various external activities, promptly seeing to transport, tickets and so on for them. Are others reluctant to attend, but worried that they may cause offence? Stress that everything is optional and indicate alternatives.

Are all the social activities now well ordered and of a suitable length?

Their order   Are they structured sensibly? Proceeding logically? Still room for improvement, though? Are some delegates late for the initial business session on the first day? Bring forward a break to open the second day allowing time to arrive, relax and socialize. Are participants unenthusiastic about an activity scheduled at the end of the event? Change its timing.

Their length   Are they well matched to the business activities? Complementary, rather than contrasting or intrusive? If lunch is set to overrun, invite speakers and delegates to take their coffees with them into the conference room so the next session can commence punctually. If a coach trip is running behind schedule cut out one of the stops, perhaps, or recommend a short cut back to the venue.

Sending everyone home

Obviously, your final duty at the event is to ensure that everyone goes home as arranged and in the right mood, and that everything is tidied up behind them – sometimes easier said than done!

Have arrangements been made for speakers and their partners to leave at the end of the conference?

When do they have to be out of their rooms? 10 a.m.? Midday? Do they know? Remind them, if necessary! What happens if items are left behind? Will they be given to you, perhaps? Tell them to check before they depart.

Does your responsibility cease as soon as they set off? What happens if their transport breaks down on their journey? Can you help them? Are they being driven home, by taxi perhaps? Is everyone aware of the arrangements? Do standby arrangements exist?

What about delegates and their partners? Have similar arrangements been made for them, too?

Is the time when they should vacate their rooms known by everyone? If not, it is your job to tell them. Lost property and the like? Check before they leave. Anything left behind should be collected from you. *Never* forward items unrequested – imagine the possible consequences if a delegate's partner at the event was not his or her spouse!

What about travel arrangements? Are people making their own way home? Again, when does your responsibility end? Now? When they arrive at their destination? Are emergency procedures in place just in case? Are you having them transported, by coach, possibly? Are the arrangements known to all parties? Has a fallback position been prepared, if problems arise?

How about arrangements with the venue at the close of the event?

When must speakers and delegates be out of the rooms? Promptly at one p.m., perhaps? Is everyone aware of this? Make sure they are. When do they have to be off the premises? Within half an hour, perhaps? Move them out on time. You may have to pay extra if they are not!

When should your equipment and other facilities and services be removed from the conference rooms? When must they be off the site completely? Again, make certain they are moved punctually to avoid incurring excess charges.

Have arrangements all been made with your suppliers?

Do individuals, such as translators, interpreters and security staff, know when their duties come to an end? What they must do at that point? Clear up behind themselves as appropriate and leave at the agreed time?

Are organizations, such as designers, equipment hirers and others who have items at the venue and/or overnight accommodation at the close of the event well aware that these items must be collected swiftly, otherwise charges will be levied – on them?

What about the overnight accommodation?

Is the hotel going to offer some leeway if participants, such as disabled guests, are a little late in leaving? Can you check the rooms before you leave so that any items left behind can be taken with you?

Do you have any equipment, facilities and services in the rooms which need to be removed? When? By whom? If by specialists, make sure hotel staff know they should not touch it. Are outsiders ready to move in to do this, if necessary?

Recommended reading

Johnson, S. (1994), *Ready-made Activities for Customer Care Skills*, Pitman, London.

Linton, I. (1995), *25 Tips for Customer Service*, Pitman, London.

Martin, D. (1994), *Dealing with Demanding Customers*, Pitman, London.

14
Following Through

Once the conference has ended it is tempting to try to return to your usual tasks and duties at the earliest opportunity. However, there is still work to be done at this late stage – and it is just as important as your earlier activities, if not more so. You need to review the event, write a report and look ahead to the future to make certain that forthcoming conferences are as successful as they can be.

Reviewing the event

Often, a conference is judged to be a success or a failure without any detailed assessment being carried out at all – typically, it is considered to be successful if participants seemed happy and satisfied, and unsuccessful if they did not. Clearly, this is inadequate – it is essential that an event is reviewed carefully and thoroughly so that more objective conclusions can be reached about its strengths, weaknesses and the consequences of staging it.

Should you analyse the early stages when you were planning to organize the conference?

Your objectives   Who, what, when, where, why and how? Have you achieved them all? If not, why? Can you identify the reasons – you need to be able to! In retrospect, were they all relevant? If not, what should your objectives have been?

The budget   Did you establish one? Was it comprehensive and sufficient for your needs? Did you adhere to it? If not, why was this? How about the cashflow forecast? Did you compose one? Was it complete and satisfactory too? Were you able to maintain it? If not, can you identify the reasons?

Your programme   Did you have a theme? Was it persuasive? Did it help you to put across your key message? Enable you to build a solid, lasting impression of the event? If not, why not? What about the business contents? Were they all relevant *and* interesting? Well balanced? Relatively brief? Were the social contents suited to the participants? Did they complement the business contents?

The schedule   Did all the planned activities unfold as expected, in the correct order and at the right times? If not, why not? Can you spot the reasons – you should be able to! Did you have enough time to do everything properly? Were some activities rushed and others omitted, perhaps? If so, why was this?

Your venue   Did you pick a good location? Was it attractive and convenient to everyone? Was there sufficient public transport and enough to do there? Did you choose a good venue and overnight accommodation? Were they easy to reach and find? Were they the right sizes? Did the facilities and services offer everything you required at value-for-money prices?

How about the build-up to the event?

Speakers   Did you pick the right ones? Were they experts, fully familiar with their subject? Were they experienced and capable and a draw for delegates? Did they do a good job? Put across the correct message? Help you to achieve your objectives? If not, why was this? Did you find and sign up speakers in the most appropriate manner and handle them properly from start to finish? Is there anything you should have done differently?

Delegates   Were the right ones there – those who will have benefited from it? Who will have helped you to achieve your goals? Who needed to be invited for political reasons? Have they done what you wanted them to do – improved their performance or placed orders? Did you draw up a contacts list and approach delegates correctly? If not, how should you have done it?

Publicity   Did you publicize your event successfully – through press releases, via direct mail or by advertising in the press? Do you think you reached the right audience? Did you put over your message and at a cost-effective price? Do you feel you achieved your objectives – to attract more delegates, perhaps? If not, why not?

Outsiders   Did you commission appropriate outside individuals and organizations to help you? Were they reputable and trustworthy? Did they have sound knowledge and experience and an interest in your requirements? Were their prices competitive? Did they do their share of the workload, and do it well? Did you find, negotiate and work with them successfully? Yes? No?

You   Was your particular role a success? Did you take an overview? Were you aware of exactly what you were doing? Did you prepare thoroughly for the conference? Did you rehearse what you were going to say and do? Did you do a good job, perform your activities well and achieve what you intended to?

Equipment   Was the right equipment, such as visual aids or audio-visual aids, used at the event? Was the best use made of them – to help you put across a speech more effectively, save time, add variety and style and ensure a message is retained for longer? If not, why?

Rehearsals   Did you coordinate everyone and everything well – speakers, delegates, the venue, the suppliers, the overnight accommodation? Did you supervise everything properly – the business programme, the social programme, the venue, the facilities and services, the overnight accommodation? Did you make any last-minute changes? If so, were these amendments effective?

Should you evaluate the conference itself?

The beginning   Did you get everyone there on time and in a positive frame of mind? Speakers? Delegates? Partners? Was everything in place for them on their arrival? Were proper arrangements made with suppliers, the venue and at the overnight accommodation?

The middle   Were the business and social activities successful? Did the speakers do well? Were all the main topics included in the sessions? Was each session approached in the most fitting manner, in the correct order and was each a suitable length?

The end Did you send speakers, delegates and partners home as arranged and in the right mood? Was everything tidied up properly behind them at the venue and at the overnight accommodation? If not, what were the reasons for this?

Who else can help you to review the event? In what ways?

Your colleagues in your firm Subordinates? Superiors, too? Whoever was involved at whatever stages may have valuable facts and opinions to share with you. Typically, superiors will have set objectives – what do they think of them now? Subordinates may have helped you at the event – what are their viewpoints?

Business contacts Your sponsors, perhaps? Your professional body? The local tourist board, if you worked with one? A convention bureau? It is worth seeking their views on their areas of involvement as and when you telephone and/or write to thank them for their help.

The venue and the overnight accommodation Is there some useful feedback available here when you contact them to acknowledge their assistance on this occasion? Is it worth asking what they think of different aspects of the conference? Can they make comments and suggestions to improve the next event you might stage there?

Speakers, delegates and partners Are they the most obvious people to approach, perhaps with a questionnaire being handed around at the close of the conference or sent out later, possibly with a thank-you letter? What did they think of the business programme, the social activities, the venue, overnight accommodation and so on? See Figure 14.1 on page 207 for an example of a participants' questionnaire.

Outside suppliers Printers? Caterers? Insurance companies? Again, can some helpful feedback be provided here as and when you telephone and/or write to thank them for their involvement? Can they supply an impartial assessment in their field, and beneficial advice?

Writing a report

Having conducted a full and thorough review of the conference, put your findings on to disk and/or paper. A detailed report of the event has many uses, both now and in the future.

Your evaluation of today

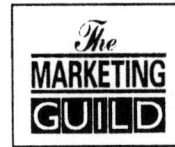

Your candid rating of today is welcomed. Future events will be changed in line with your advice. THANK YOU!

The MARKETING GUILD

Your name _____ Organisation _____

	Good	Fair	Poor
Overall value for money	☺	😐	☹
Completeness of coverage	☺	😐	☹
Overall seminar direction	☺	😐	☹
Visual aids	☺	😐	☹
Documentation	☺	😐	☹
Food & refreshments	☺	😐	☹
Administration	☺	😐	☹

Level of contents ☐ Too advanced ☐ About right ☐ Elementary

Would you recommend this event to others in your organisation? ☺ ☹

Topics *included* you would have preferred cut or omitted:

Topics *omitted* you would have preferred included or expanded:

Suggestions for improving next event:

What comments would you use to describe this seminar, if reporting it to others?

YES, we would like to quote your comments - if favourable! - in future promotional materals, but only with your permission.

My edited comments may be quoted: ☐ YES ☐ NO

THANK YOU! Please return to the Marketing Guild Ltd, 1 Houghton Court, Houghton Regis, Beds LU5 5DY. 01582 861556. Fax: 01582 864913.

Figure 14.1 Participants' questionnaire

What information should go into your conference report?

Basic facts and figures about the event   What type of event was it and what was its theme if it had a specific one? What were its purpose and objectives? Dates when it was held? The location? Details of the business and social programmes? Their timings? Who were the speakers and delegates who attended? Were fees charged? If so, how much? Anything else?

The main activities carried out   From setting objectives through to sending everyone home and thereafter? Their order? Time spent on each of them? General comments and suggestions, where appropriate – for example, reserve the venue *and* the overnight accommodation at the earliest possible moment so that you obtain exactly what you want? (See the Indexed Checklists on pages 221 to 237 to remind you of the tasks and duties that may need to be referred to.)

Your successes   Perhaps a particular speaker was enormously popular and a huge attraction to delegates? Did an advertisement in a certain publication generate a large number of first-rate responses? It is important to think about these to make sure that due consideration is given to them next time around – and to promote yourself now! Why not?

Your findings   As an example, were budgetary requirements underestimated? Perhaps the cashflow forecast was overoptimistic? Identify the reasons for these problems – inexperience, slow payers and so on. Note how they can be avoided in the future – allow for inflation, tighten financial systems and so forth – to ensure that these mistakes do not happen again.

A proviso   Stress that each and every conference is different – unique, even – and that therefore something which was successful this time may not be on a future occasion? Or vice versa – a failure now may be a success later on? So, take careful note of the report but do not follow it without reassessing a completely new set of circumstances.

How should the report be laid out?

Front page   What should this incorporate? A title, such as 'Gaythers' Sales Conference, Spring 1996'? Your name – as the author of the report? Your department and its location, as relevant? The date? Anything else you normally include at the front of your company's reports?

Contents page   Listing the various sections of the report – from its introduction right through to the appendices? Broken down into sub-sections too, for clarity and easier use? Alphabetical and numerical references, with page numbers for each of them? All as clear and as comprehensive as possible?

Introduction   Outlining the subject matter – the conference, its type, theme, objectives and so forth? Stating the purpose and scope of the report? Recording strengths and weaknesses, lessons to be learnt from mistakes, perhaps? Include who it has been commissioned by, if appropriate – the managing director, maybe? Also who it is written for – the board of directors, possibly?

Main body   Covering the core information you want to record – the key activities, successes, failings and provisos? Divided up according to your preferences? Like this text? Month-by-month in sequence? By different topics – budget, schedule and so forth? Whatever suits you, as long as it is logical and easy to follow.

Conclusions   Confirming whether main objectives were achieved or not? Summarizing the reasons for this? Consequences too, maybe? Any recommendations which may help to ensure that future conferences are 100 per cent successful – or as close to this as is possible?

Appendices   Providing detailed information which verifies and expands on data given in the report? Kept separate to avoid the main body becoming too detailed and lengthy to read easily? Forms? Typically, estimated and actual budget forms and cashflow forecasts? Graphs or charts of attendance, perhaps? Or of increased orders or sales, possibly?

What about the appearance and style of the report?

Its appearance   Is it well laid out, with plenty of self-explanatory headings and sub-headings? Are there lots of compact paragraphs, dealing with one key point at a time? Is it user-friendly with pages, headings and subheadings all numbered – and correctly! Are there ample references and cross-references – and are they all accurate? Are the appendices looking just as good, too?

Its style   Is the text clear, concise and easy to read, with short, straightforward words, sentences and paragraphs? Does it avoid jargon, clichés and 'in' expressions which date rapidly? Is it brief at all times, always keeping to the point? Does it avoid repetition – especially the tendency to mention your triumphs over and over again?

What are the main uses of your conference report?

Is its use now for internal circulation? Is it to be studied by whoever initiated the staging of the event – the board of directors, perhaps? To be read (in parts) by other interested colleagues and departments such as the accounts manager or the sales department? Is it for external circulation, to be analysed by your sponsors or your professional association, maybe? Will versions be sent to other relevant parties such as the venue, the speakers, the delegates and outside individuals and organizations who assisted you? Anyone else?

Will it be referred to later by you as and when you are asked to set up another conference? Perhaps in a year's time when your memory of this event has faded? Will it be used by a colleague or a successor who has to manage the next conference because you have been promoted or have moved elsewhere – someone who has no background knowledge and experience to draw on and who may find such a report absolutely invaluable? Has it any other uses?

Looking ahead

If you remain in your present position for the foreseeable future, then it is likely that you will be asked to organize another conference some time. Therefore, it is important that you stay in touch with this industry so you are up to date and ready to begin the whole process again, as and when required. There are numerous ways of doing this:

How much can you read about the conference industry?

It may be useful to look at magazines, such as *Conference and Exhibition Fact Finder* or similar publications such as *Conference and Seminar Selector Pack*. See 'Reference Tools' on pages 215–217 for fuller information on these titles.

What directories would it be useful for you to study? *British Conference Destinations Directory*? 'Conference Blue Book'? 'Conference Green Book'? 'Conference and Exhibition Diary', possibly? Refer again to 'Reference Tools' on pages 215–217 for further details.

Are you able to obtain information and advice from a wide variety of other sources?

Colleagues   Perhaps those below, alongside or above you in the organization? Might you obtain fresh information, perhaps from those people who have attended other events and have learned from them in some way?

Other contacts   These could include business associates, professional bodies, tourist boards, convention bureaux, and friends and relatives, even – anyone who can supply practical advice which is relevant to an ever-changing situation.

The venue   Perhaps the overnight accommodation can bring you up to date on changes and developments at their respective properties? Maybe banqueting facilities are now available on site or a new leisure complex may have been added?

Speakers, delegates and their partners   Those in particular who may have been to other conferences and seen something which can be incorporated successfully in your next one. Also, is it worth keeping in touch in case you want to invite them again?

Outsiders   These may include printers, bus and coach operators, designers, florists, equipment hirers and security firms, as well as caterers, tour operators and insurance companies. They may be able to give fresh details about their work in the industry, new hi-tech equipment now offered, or improved insurance plans. Also, it is worth maintaining contact – you may wish to deal with them again.

Trade associations   Most notably, the British Association of Conference Towns (BACT) can help with updating your information about the expanding range of locations, venues and overnight accommodation in different areas. Are there any others? See 'Useful Contacts', page 219.

Have you considered joining a trade body in this particular field? Mulled over the advantages and disadvantages of membership?

Consider those which welcome conference organizers such as you: Association of Conference Executives (ACE), Meetings Industry Association (MIA), perhaps? 'Useful Contacts' on page 219 contains fuller details of these two key associations.

The advantages of membership include prompt access to greater knowledge and experience, readily available information and advice, subsidized training courses and seminars, reference materials and so on. It also provides contact with other members operating in similar circumstances to your own, and perhaps a shoulder to lean on – or even to cry on occasionally.

The disadvantages may include the costs involved. You may also have to adhere to codes of conduct which could be a hindrance rather than a help. Membership may not be relevant to the organizer of a one-off or occasional in-house event, for example.

Have you thought about going on training courses? Considered their benefits and drawbacks?

What about those which are run by trade bodies such as the Association of Conference Executives and the Meetings Industry Association? Again, refer to 'Useful Contacts', on page 219.

The benefits may include attending highly specialized courses run by fully experienced experts in that particular field, having fresh and different attitudes, ideas and opinions applied to your individual situation and receiving up-to-date information and guidance.

There may also be drawbacks. Perhaps courses do not match your precise requirements – more theory than practice, or too specialized for your needs, perhaps? They may be expensive – especially when you add on the costs of travel, accommodation *and* lost production. Could the business suffer during your absence?

Are you ready to prepare for the next event? To begin the process again?

To plan for a successful conference   By setting appropriate objectives, establishing a realistic budget, by drafting a winning programme, planning a sensible schedule, by choosing the right venue and overnight accommodation? Yes!

To build up to the event   By bringing in first-class speakers, inviting suitable delegates, by publicizing your conference effectively, employing first-rate outsiders to assist you, by speaking well in public, using equipment satisfactorily and staging rehearsals properly? Yes!

To run the most successful conference   To achieve this with a relevant and interesting business programme supported by suitable and complementary social activities and by following through again to make a success of each and every event? Yes!

Recommended reading

Bowden, P. (1994), *How to Write a Report*, How To Books, Plymouth.
Sussams, J. E. (1994), *How to Write Effective Reports*, Gower, Aldershot.

Reference Tools

Note   The prices and other information provided here were correct at the time of going to press. Current details may be obtained from the publishers referred to.

British Conference Destinations Directory, published by the British Association of Conference Towns (BACT), First Floor, Elizabeth House, 22 Suffolk Street, Queensway, Birmingham B1 1LS, tel: 0121-616 1400, fax: 0121–616 1364.

A free, annual guide to a wide range of conference destinations throughout Britain. The entry for each individual town or city includes a description of the surrounding area, details of its conference facilities, a contact name and address plus telephone and fax numbers for further information. Well worth obtaining and reading carefully.

British Rate and Data (BRAD), published by Maclean Hunter Limited, Maclean Hunter House, Chalk Lane, Cockfosters Road, Barnet, Hertfordshire EN4 8BU, tel: 0181-975 9759, fax: 0181-440 9930.

Available at £115 for one copy or £300 for the year, this monthly, 600-page directory provides in-depth data about newspapers, magazines and numerous other media in the United Kingdom. Conference organizers intending to advertise in the press should peruse it, albeit in a library where it can be studied without charge.

Conference Green and Blue Books, published by Benn Business

Information Services Limited, PO Box 20, Sovereign Way, Tonbridge, Kent TN9 1RQ, tel: 01732 362666, fax: 01732 367301.

Regarded as the bibles of the conference industry, these two annual directories sell at £63 for the pair. The *Green Book* details conference venues, unusual locations, unconventional features and so on, while the *Blue Book* lists technical information concerning venue capacity, dimensions, lighting and so forth. Useful reads, but perhaps not worth updating every year.

Conference and Exhibition Diary, published by Themetree Limited, Prebendal Court, Oxford Road, Aylesbury, Buckinghamshire HP19 3EY, tel: 01296 28585, fax: 01296 436622.

Available on subscription at £45 per year, this is a quarterly, looseleaf publication printed in March, June, September and December. It lists conferences for the following year or more and also incorporates sections detailing event organizers and firms offering appropriate services. Helpful on a one-off subscription basis, possibly.

Conference and Exhibition Fact Finder, published by Batiste Publications Limited, Pembroke House, Campsbourne Road, Hornsey, London N8 7PE, tel: 0181-340 3291, fax: 0181-341 4840.

A monthly magazine, available on subscription at £27 per annum for United Kingdom subscribers. Its contents include general conference news, features on subjects such as recent events and refurbished venues plus a venue directory and a buyers' guide to conference facilities and services. Certainly worth subscribing to – preferably before rather than after the staging of an event.

Conference and Seminar Selector Pack. Published by Target Response, 1 Riverside, Church Street, Edenbridge, Kent TN8 5BH, tel: 01732 866122, fax: 01732 866926.

Bi-annual, free-of-charge pack containing advertising literature on a comprehensive range of conference venues, products and services. Each 'Selector Sheet' advertises a particular company – if an organizer is interested in further information he or she simply fills in their name and address, folds the sheet into an envelope and posts it back to the relevant company. Definitely worth checking, preferably at an early stage.

Directory of British Associations, Published by CBD Research Limited, 15

Wickham Road, Beckenham, Kent BR3 2JS, tel: 0181-650 7745, fax: 0181-650 0768.

An annual directory, costing £126. It lists and provides brief details about professional and trade associations across Britain. Conference organizers may wish to look at it without charge by visiting a library.

Useful Contacts

Association of Conference Executives (ACE), ACE International, Riverside House, High Street, Huntingdon, Cambridgeshire PE18 6SG, tel: 01480 475595, fax : 01480 412863.

This is a professional association with a membership of over 600 individuals and organizations who are involved in organizing, promoting, accommodating and servicing conferences and associated events. Conference organizers may wish to approach the association for help or to join it. Among the many benefits available to its members are a monthly newsletter, a what's on calendar of trade activities, and seminars and training courses at reduced rates.

British Association of Conference Towns (BACT), First Floor, Elizabeth House, 22 Suffolk Street, Queensway, Birmingham B1 1LS, tel: 0121-616 1400, fax: 0121-616 1364.

Representing more than 100 conference destinations in Britain, this association aims to support and co-ordinate its members' activities by publicizing their venues, facilities and services to a national and international audience. Of particular interest to event organizers, BACT can supply on request a complimentary directory of its members and a free venue location service. It also stages an annual exhibition in Central London, staffed by representatives of its members.

Connect, 36 Collegiate Crescent, Sheffield, Yorkshire S10 2BP, tel: 01742 683759, fax: 01742 661203.

A consortium of approximately 100 colleges and universities throughout the British Isles which offers conference services and overnight accommodation for small and large events in rural and city centre locations. Like BACT, this body provides a complimentary venue-finding service, matching organizers' requirements with the most appropriate venue available through its members.

Meetings Industry Association (MIA), 34 High Street, Broadway, Worcestershire WR12 7DT, tel: 01386 858572, fax: 01386 858986.

This is a professional body with a membership which comprises individuals and organizations who are involved in planning, managing and supplying equipment, facilities and services to the meetings industry. Conference organizers may want to contact the MIA for guidance or to become members. Membership confers numerous benefits including seminars and training programmes to help improve performance.

Indexed Checklist

Setting objectives

Establishing a budget

Drafting your programme

Planning a schedule

Choosing the venue

Bringing in speakers

Inviting delegates

Publicizing your conference

Employing outsiders

Speaking in public

Using equipment

Staging rehearsals

Managing the event

Following through

50 Essential Management Techniques

Michael Ward

Are you familiar with the concept of product life cycle? Of course you are! Does the prospect of a SWOT analysis bring you out in a cold sweat? Probably not. But what about the Johari Window? Or Zipf's Law?

Michael Ward's book brings together a formidable array of tools designed to improve managerial performance. For each entry he introduces the technique in question, explains how it works, then goes on to show, with the aid of an entertaining case study, how it can be used to solve an actual problem. The 50 techniques, including some never before published, are grouped into eleven subject areas, ranging from strategy to learning.

For managers in every type of organization and at any level, as well as for students and consultants, *50 Essential Management Techniques* is likely to become an indispensable source.

| 1995 | 240 pages | 0 566 07532 6 |

Gower

Gower Handbook of Marketing

4th Edition

Edited by Michael J Thomas

This new edition of a well-established Gower Handbook has been extensively revised and updated. Numerous chapters have been added, on subjects as diverse as relationship marketing and international marketing research, and there are many new contributors.

Part I reflects the need for a strategic view of the marketing function and looks in detail at information systems, planning, environment analysis and competitor analysis. Part II covers the organization of marketing, including recruitment, training, brand management and finance. Part III looks at product development (including services), and Part IV with distribution. The final Part examines a number of aspects of marketing where new developments are making a profound impact and casts fresh light on such familiar topics as advertising, sales promotion, direct mail and franchising.

The 36 contributors represent an immense range of expertise. They are all acknowledged leaders in their chosen field, with practical experience of marketing.

1995   672 pages   0 566 07441 9

Gower

The "How To" Guide for Managers

John Payne and Shirley Payne

- **Encourage your team to suggest their own objectives**
- **Prevent fires rather than fight them**
- **Decide! You'll never have all the information you would like**

These, and another 107 "ideas", form the basis of John and Shirley Payne's entertaining book. Whether you're newly promoted or an old hand at managing, it will help you to improve your performance and avoid some of the pitfalls you may not even have been aware of.

Written in a practical, no-nonsense style, the Guide focuses in turn on the eleven key skills of management, including setting objectives, decision making, time management, communication, motivating, delegating and running effective meetings. A questionnaire at the beginning enables you to identify those chapters that will give you the maximum benefit. Or read through the whole book - as the authors say, using their ideas can't guarantee success, but it will increase your chances.

1996   150 pages   0 566 07726 4

Gower

Project Leadership
2nd Edition

Wendy Briner, Colin Hastings and Michael Geddes

The bestselling first edition of this book broke new ground by focusing on the leadership aspects of project management rather than the technical. This radically revised edition is substantially reorganized, to introduce much new material and experience and bring the applications up to date.

Project leaders now exist in many different types of organizations, and they and their projects extend far wider than the construction work where traditional project management began. This new edition begins by explaining why the project way of working has been so widely and enthusiastically adopted, and provides new material on the role and key competences of project leaders in a wide range of different organizations. The authors provide invaluable guidance to senior managers struggling to create the context within which project work can thrive as well as be controlled. A new section, 'Preparing the Ground' reflects their increased emphasis on getting projects off to the right start, with new insights into the scoping process designed to ensure all parties agree on objectives. It also demonstrates the importance of understanding the organizational and political factors involved if the project is to succeed in business terms.

Part III shows how to handle the issues that arise at each stage of the project's life including a whole new section on the critical process of project team start up. The final section contains a thought-provoking "action summary" and a guide to further sources of information and development.

Project leadership and the project way of working has moved on. This book will provide both a conceptual framework and a set of practical tools for all those who find themselves permanently or occasionally in the project leader role, as well as an invaluable guide to setting up and maintaining project activity.

1996   192 pages   0 566 07714 0 Hardback   0 566 07785 X Paperback

Gower